CW01499911

YORK

AT WAR 1939–45

For My Parents

YOUR TOWNS & CITIES IN WORLD WAR TWO

YORK

AT WAR 1939–45

CRAIG ARMSTRONG

Pen & Sword
MILITARY

AN IMPRINT OF PEN & SWORD BOOKS LTD.
YORKSHIRE - PHILADELPHIA

First published in Great Britain in 2022 by
Pen & Sword Military
an imprint of
Pen & Sword Books Ltd
Yorkshire – Philadelphia

ISBN 978 1 52670 472 6

The right of Craig Armstrong to be identified as Author of this work has been
asserted by him in accordance with the Copyright, Designs and Patents Act 1988.

A CIP catalogue record for this book is
available from the British Library.

Typeset by SJmagic DESIGN SERVICES, India.
Printed and bound in the UK by CPI Group (UK) Ltd, Croydon, CR0 4YY.

Pen & Sword Books Limited incorporates the imprints of Atlas, Archaeology,
Aviation, Discovery, Family History, Fiction, History, Maritime, Military, Military
Classics, Politics, Select, Transport, True Crime, Air World, Frontline Publishing,
Leo Cooper, Remember When, Seaforth Publishing, The Praetorian Press,
Wharncliffe Local History, Wharncliffe Transport, Wharncliffe True Crime and
White Owl.

For a complete list of Pen & Sword titles please contact
PEN & SWORD BOOKS LIMITED
47 Church Street, Barnsley, South Yorkshire, S70 2AS, England
E-mail: enquiries@pen-and-sword.co.uk
Website: www.pen-and-sword.co.uk

Or
PEN AND SWORD BOOKS
1950 Lawrence Rd, Havertown, PA 19083, USA
E-mail: Uspen-and-sword@casematepublishers.com
Website: www.penandswordbooks.com

Contents

Introduction

York is an ancient and scenic city situated at the confluence of the Rivers Ouse and Foss and the city is home to a great number of heritage sites and buildings of historical interest. In the 19th century the city found additional fame as a major railway centre when George Hudson based his York and North Midland Railway company there. By the beginning of the 20th century the city was home to the headquarters of the North Eastern Railway (which employed more than 5,000 people).

York's other main industry was the confectionary trade with two major firms in the city. Rowntree's Cocoa Works was set up in 1862 and was later joined by Terry's of York. The two firms would later play an important role in the war.

During the late 1930s the local authorities in York were keenly aware that their city might be a target in the event of war and in 1937 discussions began about how an Air Raid Precautions group could be set up. One of the key aspects of the proposed scheme was a city-wide blackout and several rehearsals were held during which, in a precursor of what would happen during the war, a small number of people were hurt in various accidents.

When war did come many people had come to believe that York would not in fact be a major target. The city did not have a reputation for industries such as heavy engineering or armaments but, despite this, the ARP scheme still went ahead, although it was plagued with early problems. At the start of the war the city took delivery of some 1,500 Anderson Shelters while maps showing the location of the twenty-three air raid shelters in the city were distributed.

The industries which were based in York, however, did play a role in the national war effort. As a major railway hub York saw thousands of service personnel and many tons of freight pass through it on a regular basis and the city's railway station became a familiar sight to many servicemen and women. The confectioners also played a role. Their traditional industry had been badly hit by rationing of sugar and confectionaries and so they adapted. A large portion of the Rowntree's site became home to the Army Pay Corps while the cream department began manufacturing munitions alongside Ryvita and dried egg. The gum department, meanwhile, was put to work as a secret fuse factory named County Industries. The Terry's factory played host to a shadow factory of F. Hills & Sons who were making propeller blades for the Air Ministry.

One of the most noticeable changes that the war brought to the people of York was the presence of thousands of servicemen and women in the city and the surrounding area. The countryside around York was ideal for the establishment of airfields for the use, primarily, of RAF Bomber Command which, for much of the war, was the only force which was capable of taking the war to Germany. York found itself surrounded by such airfields including Driffield, Elvington, Full Sutton, Linton-on-Ouse, and Pocklington.

The air crew from these stations all made a bee-line for York when they were given leave and the city's pubs, hotels and cafes quickly became used to the sight of RAF personnel as well as those of the many airmen who had come from abroad to fight. There were a great many airmen from the Royal Canadian Air Force (RCAF), the Royal Australian Air Force (RAAF) and the Royal New Zealand Air Force (RNZAF). By 1944 they were joined by the airmen of the Free French Air Force when two squadrons took up residence at RAF Elvington. One of the most popular places for visiting airmen was the basement bar of Betty's Café and a large number scratched their names into the massive mirror there.

The presence of the air crews in York meant that the citizens could not help but be painfully aware of the realities of the war. A great number of York families became friends with particular crews only for the men to subsequently be lost on operations and this caused a great deal of grief in the city. The presence of the bombers also brought danger and there were several incidents when stricken aircraft crashed in York or in the nearby countryside.

The RAF also took over York Municipal Aerodrome which became RAF Clifton. The airfield was home to a number of squadrons, largely from RAF Army Cooperation Command, and also to 48 Maintenance Unit (48 MU) whose role was to repair the many aircraft damaged on raids mounted by Bomber Command. Large hangars were erected and the unit often had between 30-40 Halifax bombers in for repair at any given time.

York also had a proud military tradition and local regiments such as the King's Own Yorkshire Light Infantry, the Green Howards, the East Riding Yeomanry and the West Yorkshire Regiment all recruited widely from the city. In 1944 the West Yorks played a leading role in raising the siege of Imphal in Burma and as a result the Fulford Army Barracks had its name changed to Imphal Barracks. A great many York men volunteered to serve with the Army during the war while others preferred the RAF or the Royal Navy.

Like many British cities, York also had an adopted ship in the Royal Navy. HMS *York* was a heavy cruiser which had been launched at Jarrow in 1928. During the war she escorted Atlantic convoys before playing a role in the disastrous Norway Campaign in 1940. Later that year she was transferred to the Mediterranean but in 1941 she was attacked and sunk by Italian explosive motorboats. Her loss came as a blow to the people of York, many of whom had followed her career throughout the war.

In 1942, however, York suffered a severe blow when the Luftwaffe selected the city as a target for one of its Baedeker raids (which targeted towns and cities of great cultural heritage). In a large raid the city suffered massive damage with fires raging out of control. All across York there were scenes of devastation with schools, churches, shops and houses being destroyed including the historic Guildhall. Almost 100 people lost their lives in York on this horrific night.

CHAPTER 1

Civilians at War

The creation of a functional Air Raid Precautions service was fraught with complications and very often resulted in disorganisation in which services suffered due to a lack of adequate focus and direction. One of the problems which arose was the sheer cost of organising ARP services across the whole of Britain. Councils set up Emergency Committees to oversee the development and running of ARP schemes (in October 1939 York Council expanded their Emergency Committee to five members) but often these committees preferred to secure the service of as many full-time paid officers as possible to organise and run the service. Costs quickly spiralled out of control, however, and the regional controllers for civil defence were urged to rein in spending within their individual areas.

The North Eastern Regional Controller, Lord Harlech, shared the government's concerns over the amount being spent on wages for full-time officers and he visited a special meeting of the York Emergency Committee in October 1939 to discuss this and other problems within the city's ARP scheme. While Lord Harlech agreed in principle with the scaling back of expenditure in some areas, he was fully cognisant of the fact that Yorkshire was a vulnerable area close to the east coast and therefore liable to raiding and possible invasion. He had some sympathy with the local councils but also was under orders to restrict the growth of expenditure.

York's ARP scheme was further hampered by disagreements between the appointed ARP Controller (Lieutenant Colonel V.A.H. Daly), the chair of the Emergency Committee (Alderman C.T. Hutchinson), and a member of the committee (Councillor A.G. Watson), and the majority of the rest of the council. Following the meeting which Lord Harlech attended on 17 October 1939 the matters of the employment and pay of certain full-time officials reached a head and, as a result of these disagreements, Colonel Daly, Alderman Hutchinson and Councillor Watson resigned from their positions in the ARP organisation. Colonel Daly told the press that his position had been made impossible. He appeared to think that the orders of the Minister of Home Security and the methods adopted by the council were at odds. In arguing this he stated that the adoption of the recommendations by the council 'definitely contravened the orders of the Government' and that, as a result, he could not accept the responsibility which was entailed in his duties and that the 'city will not be in a state of preparedness'. Colonel Daly believed that it was 'impossible' for him to 'serve two masters – the Corporation and the Minister of Home Security'.

There had been other significant problems within the ARP scheme. Alderman Hutchinson as chair of the ARP Emergency Committee had reluctantly moved the adoption of a recommendation by the Emergency Sub-Committee that the council should not erect surface shelters and that any further adoption of surface shelters should be refused. He argued that while the city had applied for an allocation of 1,500 Anderson shelters this would still leave some 8,000 houses where it would be impossible to erect them. The council had previously approved the construction of surface shelters for these houses, with much of the cost being covered by the government, meaning that the corporation would only be paying £2 per shelter, but the Emergency Sub-Committee had turned this down. Councillor A.G. Watson moved that the shelters should be built and this was seconded by Councillor B. Cohey. Colonel P. Warren stated that he believed that the Emergency Sub-Committee had been influenced in its decision by a recent broadcast in which the Deputy Director of Home Security had said that such shelters were not needed and that the best place was the home. Alderman Hutchinson argued against this by producing a section of the broadcast in which it was stated that homes could be used to shelter from splinters but that this had been misinterpreted by the sub-committee. The vote approved the construction of surface shelters and overturned the Emergency Sub-Committee.

Another source of controversy centred around those who were employed in ARP. Alderman Dobbie asked how many full and part-time workers were employed within the city and how many of the salaried members had been previously unemployed. He suspected that they had been ignored in favour of those already in employment. Alderman Hutchinson informed his fellow alderman that 381 people were employed in ARP (the government allowed for 585) and that the majority of those employed on a full-time basis had been obtained via the Labour Exchange.

In an effort to curtail the powers of the Emergency Sub-Committee, the meeting of the ARP Committee broke up with a resolution being passed that although the sub-committee was allowed full powers to deal with any emergencies and to incur such expenses as were necessary, any particularly large expenditures should be referred to the full ARP Committee and, if possible, the council.

The Emergency Committee adjourned to consider the resignations of the three men, but the matter was clearly a serious one. On the one hand was the allegation from the city's ARP Controller, backed by the chair and a member of the Emergency Committee, that York was not prepared and would not be able to cope with an air raid; on the other hand was the clearly unaffordable expense of maintaining so many full-time ARP workers at rather high rates of salary. Daly was the former commander of the depot of the West Yorkshire Regiment and had retired on half-pay a considerable time before his appointment as ARP Controller in April 1939. He had overseen the initial founding of the city's ARP scheme, but it had been fraught with problems and criticism and at £450 per annum many thought the services of the colonel were retained at too high a rate.

Despite the controversy which was raging within the council over the organisation of the city's ARP service, the training of the members of the ARP had to go on. On Sunday, 22 October 1940 a large operation had been planned to test the strength of the services and, in particular, their reaction to a large number of casualties, but this had to be called off after those who were taking part were given warning that a preliminary air raid warning had been sounded by the regional authorities.

Days later the remaining members of the Emergency Committee and the wider council agreed to accept the resignation of Colonel Daly but had, in the meantime, convinced the other two men to resume their duties. The vacancy as Controller was filled by York's Town Clerk, Mr T.C. Benfield.

While York City Council argued over the city's ARP scheme there were other concerns amongst the city's teachers. The closure of schools, many of which had been taken over by the ARP services due to lack of shelter provision was a source of controversy. The York and District Teachers' Association passed on a resolution to the education committee which had been unanimously agreed by over 250 members and which expressed alarm at the 'continued closure of many schools in the city and the consequent complete loss of educational facilities for a large proportion of the children'. It urged the re-opening of schools without shelters where headteachers could establish with the council and with parents safe schemes for the dispersal of children in the event of an air raid warning.[1] While this was absolutely understandable it was also unrealistic and would have been against government policy for such a proposal to have been adopted.

The system of rationing which was introduced in January 1940 was obeyed by most but there was an active black market and the very nature of the law did tend to criminalise some otherwise law-abiding people for minor transgressions or mistakes and the authorities were keen to make an example of alleged lawbreakers. On 18 March York's food control authorities brought their first prosecution when a butcher's stallholder at York market was prosecuted for having sold bacon without taking the relevant ration coupons. Mr C.W. Pye-Bayley of Castle Road, Scarborough, was accused of having sold 2½ lbs of bacon to an observer on one occasion on 21 February and 3½ lbs to another observer. Mr Pye-Bayley's legal representative argued that on that weekend his client had been exceptionally busy and had 1,200 registered customers along with 200 who were unregistered for the buying of off-ration 'boiling parts'. The busyness of the weekend and the fact that the alleged offences had occurred so long ago meant that his client had no recollection of the particular customers. Despite the fervour of the prosecuting authorities the magistrates appear to have been sympathetic and understanding of the difficulties in Mr Pye-Bayley's case and found him not guilty, dismissing both charges.

The blackout restrictions which were applied to motor-vehicles led to a spate of accidents, especially during the winter months. In the early hours of 23 March 1940 Mr John Grisdale (37), a well-known York agricultural valuer, was driving home from Doncaster when he was involved in a collision with another car near to the South Milford and Monk Fryston crossroads. The other car contained Major H.E. Barker, his wife and Second Lieutenant Michael Smithson. All of those involved were injured to one extent or another and taken to hospital in Leeds. Major Barker sustained a broken arm and leg in addition to facial wounds, his wife rib injuries and a broken wrist and Second Lieutenant Smithson concussion and lacerations to the face and leg. The most seriously injured, however, was Mr Grisdale who sustained a fractured skull and arm. Unfortunately, despite the best efforts of the hospital staff Mr Grisdale succumbed to his injuries shortly after admission. Mr Grisdale had grown up at Toll Garth, Dringhouses and for a number of years had farmed at Sheriff Hutton before becoming an employee of Messrs Thomlinson & Son, auctioneers and agricultural valuers.

At the end of May 1940 the rash of road accidents during the blackout claimed another York victim, Thomas Dingsdale, a well known former star player for York Rugby League FC. On the night of 30/31 May he had been travelling along the Tadcaster road when his car came off the road, fell down an embankment and came to rest on the main rail line. The car was then struck by the King's Cross to Aberdeen express and carried for a distance of quarter of a mile. Mr Dingsdale had been thrown clear of the car but was killed while his two companions, Edmund Spillane (captain of Bramley RLFC) and Mr Desmond Day from York, were rescued from the wreckage by a police officer and a civilian.

One of the problems facing York (and many other northern towns and cities) was that of inadequate and poor housing. At the beginning of August 1940 a case was brought before the magistrates which highlighted these deficiencies. Mrs Frances Taylor of Earswick had previously lived in a house with her husband and daughter but (for unknown reasons) she had been forced by her landlady, Mrs Moore, to move across the road to live in a converted railway carriage which was also owned by Mrs Moore. The carriage was judged by the local authority, Flaxton Rural Council, to be suitable for at the most three occupants but a visiting sanitary inspector had seen that the carriage was in fact occupied by the Taylors and their daughter, and two married daughters, Mrs Longmore and Mrs Kilshaw, and their four children. This was a clear case of overcrowding and the case was brought before the magistrates. Despite the pleas of Mrs Taylor that she was attempting to find a suitable house but had been unsuccessful, the court, rather harshly, fined her (Mr Taylor was not mentioned) the sum of £1 for causing a dwelling-house to be overcrowded. Mrs Moore claimed that she had given Taylor notice to quit the property and that the tenant had agreed to do so, but the magistrates were unmoved and she was fined the lesser sum of 15s for permitting the overcrowding and was admonished for not reporting the tenants when they failed to leave.

The ARP service in York had its first real test on the night of 11 August when a small number of Luftwaffe bombers attacked the Yorkshire area.[2] By this time there were some 1,000 ARP wardens serving in the city and they were quickly called to their duty stations. There had been some warning that the area might be attacked that night as a Junkers Ju88 was shot down near Whitby while flying a reconnaissance sortie. In the event only a handful of bombs fell in the vicinity of York. One bomb hit the park area of York cemetery. No graves were destroyed although several headstones suffered damage along with the windows of the chapel which were blown out. Close to the cemetery a bomb blew out several windows and caused property damage to a number of shops and houses as well as a Methodist chapel. Another bomb landed between Clifford's Tower and Piccadilly but failed to explode. Two more bombs fell in the suburbs but caused limited damage; one fell into a hedge bottom while the other exploded in a potato field. A policeman who was standing in his front path was knocked from his feet, an elderly woman was left shocked after the windows of her house were blown in and another had her ceiling fall in while she was eating supper.

York ARP Wardens. Back row, left to right: Newby, J. D. Holmes, A. L. Pearson, Col. I.N. Ware, A. Murphy, J. Donaldson, A. Hudson, G. Dwson, Councillor H.C. Deburgh; Front row, left to right: Birkett, C. J. Minter, H. Richardson, T. C. Benfield, R. S. Oloman, G. H. Hunt, R.B. Wright, E. Hardisty, W.G. Birch. (York Libraries and Archives)

The Archbishop of York (William Temple) proved to be a contentious figure throughout the war and, although many of his opinions found little favour with the majority of the British public and the government, in mid-August 1940 he weighed into the debate surrounding conscientious objection. Temple had become aware that several public bodies had summarily dismissed employees who had objected to military service on the grounds of being conscientious objectors. Temple regarded this practice as abhorrent, 'utterly deplorable' and unpatriotic. The fact that the country was fighting for freedom meant, to him, that freedom of conscience, which had been acknowledged by the government, was an indivisible right. Temple did, however, support the proposal that any man who avoided service due to his conscience should not be better off than if he was serving in the services, but he should not face dismissal from his employment. Temple's opinions found some favour with the more liberal sections of society (as well as some communists) but the vast majority of the population were unmoved by his moral stance and were unwilling to show much sympathy to conscientious objectors.

Temple also spoke at some length on the topic of the internment of enemy aliens. Yet again, his views were unlikely to find mass support. He acknowledged that the government had been left with no choice but to round up and intern these people following the invasion of Holland and the Low Countries and that there was bound to be some initial hardship involved due to the rapid nature of the action and the need to assess the internees, but argued that the improvements in conditions for the internees had been far to slow. Temple acknowledged that officials were very hard-pressed but stated that the current state of affairs reflected badly upon the country and was causing 'acute suffering for many of our true friends'.[3]

The remainder of 1940 passed relatively quietly for the residents of York. Work continued apace in the local factories and many young men and women took the opportunity to volunteer for service with one of the armed forces, but there was little enemy activity over the city. There was one particular alarm in November when a single bomb landed beside the city's waterworks but the soft ground upon which the bomb landed meant that the explosion was contained and did very little damage.

Although York had so far escaped serious or concerted attack the authorities were under no illusions that the city was not a viable target and preparations to cope with raiding continued. After the war this caution was justified when a Luftwaffe target map was recovered which showed potential targets in York, marked upon aerial photos of the city. The main targets included the railway station and the Terry's factory, but also the Minster.

Raiding in the North-East during 1941 had resulted in a heightened awareness of the importance of the ARP workers and many organisations banded together to raise further funds for them. In August 1941 the York Girl Guides and Brownies managed to raise £80 in just six weeks to fund the purchase of a mobile canteen. After they had collected the money the girls gifted it to the WVS and it was jointly decided to purchase the mobile canteen as a gift from both groups. The chairman of York ARP Committee, Alderman C.T. Hutchinson, accepted the gift gratefully and, after expressing his thanks, said that the canteen would be used primarily to feed ARP workers and firemen after a raid, but would also be used to give aid to those who had been bombed out of their houses.

On 25 July 1941 Mr James Wilson Reid (38), an engineer from Wheatlands Grove, appeared before York magistrates charged with two serious allegations under the Defence Regulations. Although Mr Reid's solicitor asked that his client be granted bail, adding that this was a democratic country and his client should be treated as anyone else having agreed to report to the police twice daily. The police, however, strongly opposed this with Superintendent Williams telling magistrates that Reid, who was, or had been, a member of the British Union of Fascists (BUF), posed a threat to the safety of the realm and that the police had been monitoring his movements and knew that he had not been staying at home for some time. Magistrates agreed and remanded

Luftwaffe target map of York. (Bundesarchiv, Koblenz)

Reid. The trial of Captain James Ramsay, MP, was ongoing at the time and the paranoia about members of the BUF was rife.

By 11 August, Mr Reid was making his fifth appearance before the magistrates. At this hearing the magistrates were told by the Director of Public Prosecutions that the trial would be further delayed as witnesses from the War Office had to be traced. Once again, Mr Reid's solicitor asked for bail, saying that his client had already been remanded for some time and the case appeared interminable, while Mr Reid himself argued that all he had done was attempt to gain a commission, adding that he had not asked for it but had been offered it and that he had 'done nothing against my country'.[4]

On 21 August Mr Reid appeared before York magistrates for the seventh time, charged with two offences under the Defence Regulations Act and two under the Forgery Act. Reid's case was fixed for 25 August as the prosecution was bringing witnesses from as far afield as London. Mr Reid thanked the police for attempting to find witnesses for himself but told the magistrates that they had not managed to do much and he once again requested bail so he could find witnesses as otherwise, he claimed, he would be entering his trial without any defence. He added that he had 'a jolly good answer to this case',[5] but the magistrates once again refused bail and Mr Reid was remanded into custody.

When Reid came to court the Director of Public Prosecutions laid before him the charges, namely, that he had written to the War Office in order to apply for a commission in the Royal Army Ordnance Corps (RAOC) in January. He had subsequently been interviewed and sent application forms in which he was expected to submit the names of two people who had known him for at least four years, who were serving or retired officers or businessmen of good standing, and who could vouch for his good character. Reid had submitted his application on 7 March with his references coming from a Mr Mooney and a Dr Burrows. Letters were sent to the two men but, although Mr Mooney replied satisfactorily, Dr Burrows wrote that he had no recollection of ever having met Mr Reid. At the request of the War Office Mr Reid was asked to submit an alternate referee and submitted the name of C. Christian, a consulting engineer of 19 De Gray Street, York. A reply was subsequently received in which Mr Christian signed himself as C. Christian DFC, AMIME, and in which he stated that Reid was 'the type of man the country has need for in the present emergency'. This satisfied the War Office and Reid was accepted onto the Officers' Emergency Reserve. On 12 May the War Office offered Mr Reid a commission but, days later, information was received that Mr Christian barely knew Reid, was not a DFC or an AMIME (an unknown 'award'), and that Reid had intercepted the letter and arranged for the testimonial to be typed by someone else. The offer of a commission was therefore withdrawn.

The police visited Reid, who admitted forging the signature on the reference letter and on 25 July the police applied for and were granted a search warrant. The subsequent search recovered a BUF shirt and belt and a picture of Reid wearing the shirt. Mr Reid's solicitor objected to this evidence being presented, saying that it was irrelevant to the case and that the magistrates were being bullied into accepting a false picture of his client. The Director of Public Prosecutions retorted by saying that it was 'a matter for the magistrates to consider with what object this man endeavoured to obtain a commission in the Forces'.

The second set of charges related to the allegation that Mr Reid had attempted to obtain work at an RAF station in July and that, as part of this attempt, he had submitted a form in which he claimed Mr Christian was his former employer and that a subsequent reference request had been, once again, returned with a forged signature which Reid had admitted to having signed himself.

Mr Reid testified that he wished to play a more active role in the war. He had wished to be involved in the war from the start but because he was a qualified engineer the War Office would not consider him. He admitted to having forged the signature of Mr Christian but said that he had never asked for a commission but only wanted to get into the Army. In answer to the allegations regarding his membership of the

BUF, Reid said that he had joined the organisation in 1934 but had left the following year and declared that at the time he joined the BUF 'stood for King and Country, and I was very keen to do anything that was patriotic'.

Unfortunately for Reid his prior character told against him when it was revealed to the court. Reid had nineteen previous convictions against him ranging back to 1922. He had served several terms of imprisonment for fraud and false pretences. In addition to this it was 'known that he was dismissed from an aircraft factory in the North of England for sowing disaffection and defeatism among employees'.[6] Superintendent Williams described Reid as being a dangerous criminal who had a superiority complex, had no respect for authority, was boastful of his misdeeds and had used every educational and professional qualification he had received to aid his criminal career. It was also revealed that in 1931 a court at Newcastle had allowed Reid bail and he had subsequently absconded with nothing more being heard of him for a year until he appeared before a Dublin court under a false name. Unsurprisingly, the magistrates found Reid guilty of the charges against him and sentenced him to five months' imprisonment.

The many men and women who volunteered to serve in various capacities of civil defence and ARP were voluntarily placing their lives in danger as they had to work through alerts and raids. Not only that but much of their work was undertaken in the darkness of the blackout and it often involved work which was potentially dangerous. On the night of Sunday, 21 September 1941 the National Fire Service (NFS) officer in charge of the brigade's fire float was reported missing from the vessel. The body of Mr Robert Sunderland (63) was discovered in the River Ouse in the early hours of 23 September. Mr Sunderland was formerly a boatman and lived at Etty Avenue.

On Monday, 13 October 1941 the body of a widow, Mrs Theodora Greenhill was discovered in her flat in West Kensington, London. The police established that Mrs Greenhill had been strangled and that property worth £100 was missing from her home. The police also established that a man had gained entry to Mrs Greenhill's property after expressing an interest in renting the flat. Upon leaving he had hailed a taxi. A specimen of the suspect's handwriting was recovered from the flat and on 16 October a black cabin trunk and a briefcase were found in Birmingham, which contained some jewels and clothing from Mrs Greenhill's flat. In the days following the police released a description and photographs of a man they believed to be named Dr Trevor whom they wanted to question over the incident. The police alert stated that Dr Trevor spoke with a cultured accent and wore a monocle, but also that this man had been known to go by other identities including Mr Marjoribanks and Mr Atkins as well as claiming to be a military officer.

Just two days later a war reserve police officer in Rhyl saw a man matching the description and asked him to accompany him to the nearest police station. The suspect confirmed that he was the person identified and gave his name as Harold Dorien Trevor of York. The 62-year-old, whose fingerprints were found at the scene, was later found guilty of the murder and was hanged at Wandsworth on 11 March 1942.

Saturday, 15 February 1942 saw York launch its Warship Week campaign with the intention of raising some £1,250,000 to fund the hull of a cruiser to replace HMS *York* (the old cruiser had been crippled at Suda Bay at the end of March 1941 and then abandoned when the Allies evacuated Crete). The campaign was launched by Rear Admiral Laurence Oliphant. The Lord Mayor (Mrs E.A. Crichton) introduced the admiral by alluding to the fact that just that week, for the first time in more than a century, an enemy fleet had managed to pass through the Straits of Dover. She concluded that there was no lack of courage or conviction, but that there was a lack of ships. In answering her the admiral said that although a large army and air force were necessary it would be the Royal Navy that was once more the saviour of the nation. Together the two dignitaries urged the people of York to consider the amount that they had decided to lend to the campaign and then to double or even treble that amount.

In late April 1942 the magistrates once again found York engineer James Wilson Reid before them. Reid, a former member of the BUF and a career criminal with twenty-two previous convictions, had only just completed a five month sentence for two counts apiece of forgery and contraventions of the Defence Regulations. One of the conditions of his release which had been imposed by the Home Secretary was that he regularly check in with the police and notify them of his movements. Superintendent Williams alleged that for several days the accused had resided in Hull without informing the police. Mr Reid's long-suffering but persistent solicitor, Mr Paul Crombie, submitted that there was no case to answer as his client had no intention of permanently taking up residence in Hull and had been obliged to stay overnight after working overtime. This completely missed the point and, given Mr Reid's already established attitude to authority, was very unlikely to impress the magistrates. It did not, and the magistrates duly fined Reid the sum of £3 for contravening a restriction order made by the Home Secretary.

During 1942 the RAF made several unsuccessful attempts to sink the battleship *Tirpitz* while it was berthed at Norway. In June another unsuccessful attempt was made. One of the losses on this raid was the Halifax of the commanding officer of 10 Squadron (Wing Commander Don Bennett). With the plethora of bomber bases scattered in the countryside around York it was imperative that operational security be maintained, especially when special operations such as the attacks on the *Tirpitz* were being attempted. For one woman who was married to a flight sergeant in Bomber Command the temptation to use her knowledge in order to appear informed led to a court appearance.

Mrs Margaret May Alderson was charged with, between March and May, having communicated information pertaining to aircraft operations, casualties, crashes and personnel which might have been of use to the enemy. It would seem that Flight Sergeant Alderson was revealing far too much information to his wife. It was alleged that in April Mrs Alderson had visited a shop and asked the assistant if she knew any of the boys (meaning the airmen). She had then gone on to say that they were being sent to another aerodrome to undertake an operation over Norway. Other witnesses testified that during a visit to a house near to the aerodrome Mrs Alderson had spoken about a recent operation. She asked the visitors if they were aware that the wing commander had been lost on the operation but that several men had escaped capture. On yet another occasion she told a neighbour that an aircraft had crashed while on a flight to a certain airfield. Yet another witness stated that she had been on a bus when Mrs Alderson sat in the seat behind her. Mrs Alderson began talking about aircraft being moved to another aerodrome and the witness had turned around and told her that she should not be talking about such matters.

Giving evidence, an RAF intelligence officer told the court that most of the information passed on by Mrs Alderson was factually correct and that the nature of the information would have been very valuable to the enemy. When questioned Mrs Alderson said that she could remember only talking to two people and believed that she had not passed on information of any value. However, she told the court when confronted by the evidence that she recognised that she had been very foolish and that she would not repeat her indiscretions. The court found Mrs Alderson guilty of the charges brought against her and bound her over for two years in addition to ordering her to pay costs of £5 5s.

Following the raid on York at the end of April 1942 the Lord Mayor undertook an assessment of the housing situation in the city. One of the major problems caused by the raid was the further loss of valuable housing stock. By July it had been agreed that the cost of repairs would be covered by the War Damage Commission and by the Housing Committee. The Lord Mayor, who was also chair of the Housing Committee, had overseen a full review of the state of housing in the city and reported that the list of applicants who were waiting for homes stood at over 800 before the raid but that this had now increased to almost 1,000. Furthermore, there was severe overcrowding with many examples of two families sharing one property 'under very uncomfortable conditions'.[7] Despite this, the Lord Mayor concluded that officially there was no overcrowding on a basis of one person per room and per bedroom.

The Lord Mayor went on to say that the official position was that there was enough room in the city to billet the homeless but that this took no consideration of comfort or living conditions. The war had already badly stretched York's housing stock. A large number of properties which had been scheduled for demolition under pre-war slum clearance schemes had instead been fixed up and used to house evacuees from other towns and cities. Even as late as July 1942 there were almost 900 men working to repair such properties and to make them more comfortable for habitation. Despite this, there were many families who were homeless and were either being billeted with others or staying with friends in small, overcrowded, properties. In a great many cases this involved two large families living in one small property.

At the same time as the report on the city's housing stock was being delivered the Health Committee could report better news for the future of the city's children. Councillor T. Harwood informed the council that at least 7,587 of the city's estimated 20,745 children under the age of fifteen had now been immunised against diphtheria and, as a result of this, the previous six months had seen just sixty-four cases in this age group and only three amongst those who had received the injection.

July 1942 also saw some complaints over the quality of the bus services in York and the surrounding area when Norton Rural District Council wrote to York to solicit support for a letter which they were writing asking for an increase in services from Scarborough to Malton and York. The Norton councillors claimed that many passengers were being left at the roadside as the buses which were currently running were often full. The Town Clerk of York had made enquiries of the company which ran the service and had been informed that they had increased the number of vehicles (in some cases tripling availability) during the war as the route was seeing very heavy use. The company, the West Yorkshire Road Car Company, also informed the Town Clerk that the matter had been extensively discussed with the Regional

Transport Commissioner who had taken the view that everything possible had been done and no additional transport could be allowed due to the petrol rationing.

Opinion amongst York councillors was divided on the matter with Councillor Colley arguing that the situation was no worse than anywhere else and urging no action be taken, while Councillor Oliver argued that support should be given to Norton's claim as he had received reports that many York businesses were suffering a loss of trade as people from Malton and other places on the route were unable to get on the buses due to those who were making the entire journey from Leeds to Scarborough, often for reasons of leisure. Councillor Hargrave sought to shift the debate by arguing that if the council was to support Norton then it should first take action over the bus situation within York itself as he had reports that many people were being forced to miss buses which went past them as they were full. In answer to this point, Alderman Birch said that this problem was being caused by too many people boarding buses for what were very short journeys and that this was placing too much strain on the services. The situation could be eased by people acting more sensibly. Councillor De Burgh added his opinion, stating that it was a matter for the government to intervene and instruct people against travelling by bus for pleasure. When the matter was put to the vote the council decided not to act in support of Norton by eighteen votes to twelve.

At the end of July 1942 there were reports of a small number of bombs falling on the city, but damage was very limited and there were no casualties. The bombing experiences of York during this period tended to be when lone raiders penetrated the defences, or when bombers heading for other targets jettisoned their bombs in the vicinity of the city because they were in difficulties. At the beginning of August, for example, a lone German aircraft penetrated the limited defences around York and managed to drop four bombs on the city centre. Two failed to explode but those that did caused property damage, killed one person, seriously injured nine and injured a further thirty-six people less seriously. Mr Sidney Thompson (33), a member of the National Fire Service (NFS), was killed while serving on board the city's fire float at King's Staith.

News accounts of enemy raids were couched in terms which meant that little or no information was given to the enemy but this understandable censorship also frustrated people in York. It was trying when the city had been bombed for people to read the next day a vague account in which limited damage and casualties had been sustained in an unnamed North-East town or city. In the early hours of 24 September 1942, for example, a small number of raiders managed to successfully attack York. The next day the residents of the city read how an incendiary attack had been made on a North-East inland town. It would seem that, although the anti-aircraft defences quickly went into action, the alarm had failed to sound in some areas and many people were awakened when incendiaries fell onto their homes. Large numbers of people were evacuated to feeding and rest centres and there was a considerable amount of property damage. Two serious fires developed and a warehouse was destroyed, while the garage of a brewery was also gutted along with a number of lorries which were inside.

One young woman awoke to find that her bedroom was on fire. She quickly gathered up her baby and, with her pyjamas ablaze, ran downstairs where her sister managed to extinguish her clothing. Some of the bombs dropped were delayed action high-explosive types while a number of explosive incendiary bombs were also dropped. It was reported that these latter types 'popped off disconcertingly but they did not deter fire-watchers from getting on with heir jobs'.[8] Several people endeavouring to fight the fires were hurt by these bombs, however. Three people were killed in this raid. Mr Thomas Marsh (82) of 32 Aldwark died of shock, while Mr Percy Beckwith (61) died from the same condition at a rest centre. The final victim was an air raid warden, Mr Joseph Kirby (57) of 182 Stockton Lane.

In York, as across Britain, there were significant problems with young people who, having little else to occupy themselves with, were increasingly turning to mindless vandalism and petty crime. The now largely unused air raid shelters which were scattered across the city were frequent targets. Men had been employed to look after some of the shelters and the police were aware of the situation but with 450 communal shelters, 100 public shelters and numerous school shelters policing them all was an impossible task. In mid-November 1942 York City Council's Civil Defence Emergency Committee heard that despite their best efforts the vandalism was a mounting problem and that very serious damage was being done to a large number of shelters.

The Luftwaffe returned to York on the night of 17 December when enemy bombers rained down both incendiaries and high-explosive bombs. Press accounts once more sought to limit the information, merely stating that an inland town in the North-East had been attacked and that 'some damage was done'.[9] In fact, the raid had caused serious property damage and resulted in a further two deaths. A hospital was amongst the buildings to suffer damage and Mr Alfred Keech (52) was killed nearby in Hospital Lane. The other fatality was Mr Frederick Christopher Poole (34), a baker who was on his way home from work who was killed at Monkgate. Several serious fires were started and two gas holders caught fire.[10] A school was also destroyed by fire and the children were not altogether distraught at this enforced extension to their Christmas holiday. In addition to the deaths three men were seriously injured while a further eleven people were less seriously hurt.

We have already seen how the people of York had formed strong connections with the airmen who were based in the nearby countryside, but the proximity of so many bases also meant that many York residents witnessed some of the frequent accidents which claimed so many lives during the war. On 14 April 1943 the crews of Bomber Command were briefed for an operation to Stuttgart. Before operations each crew was expected to fly an air test to ensure that their aircraft was serviceable for the coming night. At RAF Leeming the crew of 26-year-old Edinburgh pilot Flying Officer C.W.G. Gray from 429 (Bison) RCAF Squadron climbed aboard Wellington X (HZ203) to fly their brief air test. Flying Officer Gray, a married man, and his crew had been in the squadron for almost exactly one month. Their aircraft was a relatively new one having flown only nine operations since its arrival at Leeming on 1 April.

Flying Officer Gray and his crew took off at 3:10pm but just one hour later as they neared the end of their air test disaster struck. As the Wellington overflew the village of Huntington on the outskirts of York at just 1,000 feet witnesses reported seeing the aircraft losing power on its engines and spinning down to earth where it crashed in some gardens before ploughing into several houses in the village close to the church. The Wellington immediately burst into flames. Flying Officer Gray and his four comrades were killed as were three elderly residents of the village. The civilian victims were in two houses named 'Rydale' and 'The Roost'. In the first house the victims were Mrs Henrietta Morley (73) and her sister Miss Clara Jane Pickard (71) while Miss Jane Raby Freer (90) was the victim in the second house. It is believed that Mrs Morley and Miss Freer were killed instantly but press reports at the time reported that Miss Pickard managed to crawl to her door where she was found dying by neighbours. 'The Roost' was owned by a Mr and Mrs Dixon and Mr Dixon had a fortunate escape as he had left the house to go for a walk shortly before the crash while his wife was in York at the time.

In mid-November 1943, the familiar face of Mr James Wilson Reid appeared once again before the magistrates. In the last two years Reid had served a five month sentence for forgery and offences under the Defence Regulations and had been fined for breaching restrictions imposed upon him by the Home Secretary. On this occasion, Mr Reid had been summonsed under charges for the illegal use of petrol. His employer, Robert McLellan, a quarry owner, appeared on his behalf and agreed to pay the £5 fine, telling the magistrate, rather hopefully given this was Reid's twenty-third conviction, that he hoped it might steer Reid onto a straight and narrow path and halt his lawbreaking.

The influx of airmen to the stations scattered around the Vale of York led to interactions between the airmen and the civilians of York and in many cases to good friendships and relationships. Many of these were of course interrupted by tragedy, particularly when they involved men who were flying with RAF Bomber Command. For the men of Bomber Command (and, indeed, a great many of the WAAFs too) the periods when they were stood down for a night or a few days almost inevitably meant a trip to York and its various pubs and dance halls. One of the most popular amongst the men of Bomber Command, and certainly the most famous, was Betty's Bar. Colloquially known amongst the aircrew as 'The Dive' the licensed premises attracted huge numbers of airmen throughout the war and proved especially popular with the Canadians of 6 Group. One of the most poignant aspects of Betty's was the huge picture mirror upon which many airmen engraved their names, often using a diamond ring borrowed from one of the staff.[11]

Betty's was also known as a place where operational details were often discussed, despite repeated warnings to the airmen. This phenomenon resulted in the premises attracting the further nickname of 'The Briefing Room'. So widespread was this that *The Tatler* even ran a cartoon emphasising the point.

On the night of 3/4 March 1944 RAF Bomber Command launched two attacks, one on the Dortmund-Ems Canal and the other on an oil refinery at Kamen. The attacks were successful but as people in York and the surrounding hinterland listened to the now very familiar sounds of heavy bombers returning to base, the night was shattered by repeated bursts of gunfire and the explosions of crashing aircraft. The Luftwaffe had mounted an operation, codenamed Gisella, using a large number of night fighters to attack RAF bombers as they prepared to land back at their bases. The operation took the British completely by surprise and in the space of under one hour at least twenty-four bombers fell victim. The night fighters also strafed ground targets as opportunity presented.

At Dunnington Lodge Farm, near Elvington, a Ju88 night fighter which had just shot down two Halifax bombers turned toward RAF Elvington

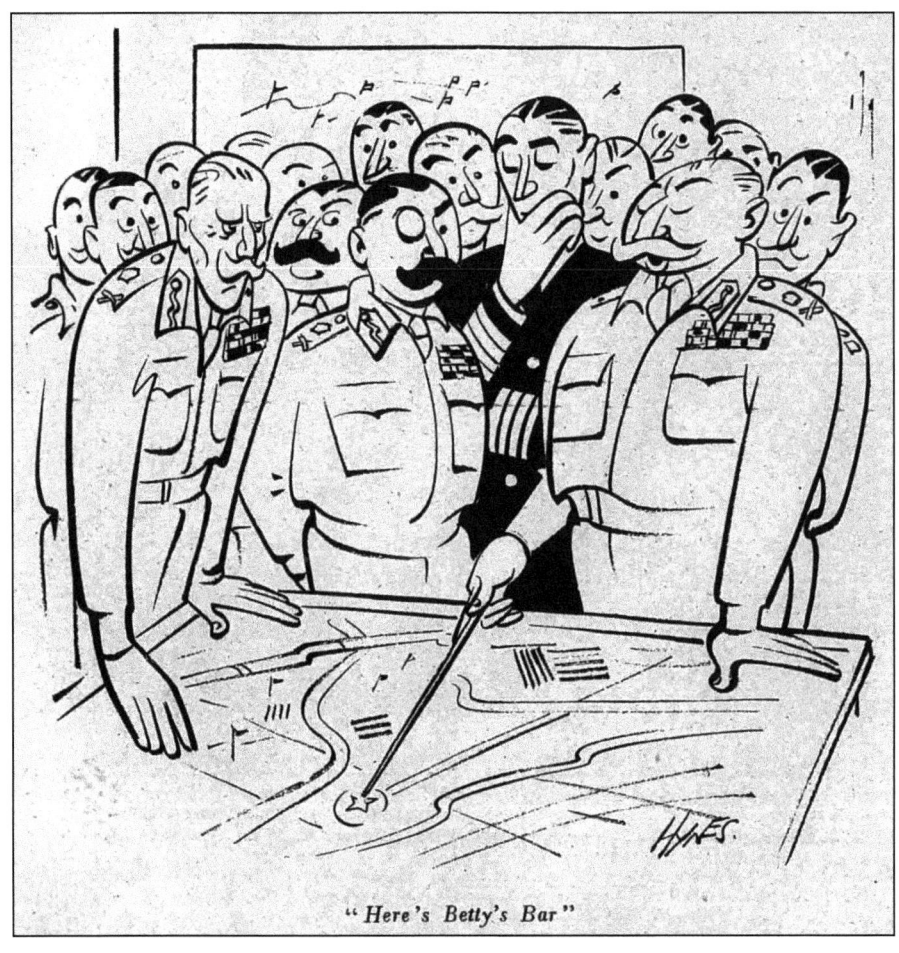

Cartoon highlighting the fame of Betty's Bar. (The Tatler)

at low level. The aircraft, however, hit a tree and crashed into the ground, hitting the farmhouse and killing three civilians in addition to the four Luftwaffe airmen. The civilian dead, all from the same family, were Richard Herbert Moll (67), his wife Ellen (61) and their daughter-in-law, Violet (28). When the aircraft crashed, Violet, who was heavily pregnant, ran to the front bedroom occupied by Mr and Mrs Moll, where all three perished along with Violet's unborn child. Violet's husband, Freddie, and a son survived the horrific incident. They were both occupying a bedroom at the rear of the property which escaped largely unscathed.

With the Soviet armies pushing German forces into retreat RAF Bomber Command was tasked with disrupting communications and oil supplies in eastern Germany and on the night of 5/6 March 1945 a large raid on Chemnitz was planned. This led to disaster and tragedy for several 6 (RCAF) Group squadrons based around York and for the civilian population in the city. As the aircraft from several RCAF squadrons circled for height over Yorkshire before setting course they ran into unforecast heavy icing conditions. Ice forming on the engines and control surfaces of the bombers resulted in several aircraft crashing while a further two Halifaxes collided in mid-air. The worst incident occurred over York itself. At RAF Linton-on-Ouse Flight Lieutenant I. Emerson, RCAF, and his crew took off at 4:39pm aboard Halifax VII (LW210, OW-Y) but very soon after take-off the bomber suffered very severe icing. After being in the air for only twenty minutes and while over York the bomber was forced into a steep dive by the ice which had formed on its wings. Witnesses in York saw the aircraft emerge from cloud and the pilot managed to level out, but almost immediately a section of the starboard wing broke off and the Halifax rolled which caused further structural failures as one of the starboard engines broke away followed by sections of both wings, the rudders and parts of the tail structure. Flight Lieutenant Emerson gave the order to abandon the aircraft but only the wireless operator managed to exit from the stricken bomber before it fell into a vertical spin, breaking up as it descended, and crashed upon several houses on Nunthorpe Grove.

The fuselage hit no.26 and no.28, utterly demolishing them and killing two elderly residents at no.28. The body of one of the aircrew was found in the grounds of Nunthorpe Secondary School for Boys and some accounts have stated that he baled out but was too low for his parachute to open. It is equally likely that this unfortunate victim, most likely one of the air gunners, was simply flung out of the disintegrating wreckage as it fell to earth. The wireless operator, Pilot Officer J. Low, RCAF, had what can only be described as a miraculous escape.

When he baled out his parachute failed to open fully, possibly because he was too low when baling out, but was inflated by the blast of one of the bombs which exploded on the ground. Pilot Officer Low then got caught up in some trees as he landed in the garden of no.29 Nunthorpe Grove. The airman struck a shed and badly injured his back. He was discovered caught up in the trees by a local plumber named Hardcastle. Mr Hardcastle immediately went for help as bombs from the aircraft continued to explode, causing severe damage to other properties, but on his return a blast hurled debris through the air and Mr Hardcastle was struck on the leg and badly injured by a manhole cover. When Pilot Officer Low was finally released he was found to have suffered a broken back and was rushed to hospital.[12]

There were many witnesses to the crash which was in a heavily populated area and locals and visitors quikly rushed to the scene to assist. Amongst the would-be rescuers were a group of RAF policemen and some soldiers who were taking part in a nearby boxing tournament. A large crowd of civilians had assembled and were attempting rescues regardless of the fact that several bombs were lying in the street and in the inferno. Alongside those who had rushed to the site, the National Fire Service (NFS) arrived and quickly began fighting the fires. Despite the massive risk from exploding bombs the firemen managed to get the blaze under control in around an hour.

Fifteen minutes after the crash a 500lb bomb exploded killing three people and injuring a number of others. Bombs continued to explode as the rescue efforts continued. Wreckage from the bomber was scattered over a wide area. The detached engine fell on the kitchen of Nunthorpe Secondary School for Boys while a bomb fell onto 42 Millfield Road and came to rest without exploding under the floor of the neighbouring property (no.44).

Once the dust had settled and the wreckage had been sorted through it was established that, in addition to the deaths of the six aircrew, five people had been killed on the ground. These included two elderly women, two soldiers and an Italian PoW. At least twenty-three people were injured including two firemen, two Italian PoWs, three soldiers and nine RAF personnel.

Those killed in the crash of the Halifax on Nunthorpe Grove, 5 March 1945

Name	Rank and Service	Age	Notes
Ivor Emerson	F/Lt, RCAF	29	Pilot
Walter Thomas Symes	P/O, RAF	21	Flight Engineer
Alick Matheson Hutchison	F/O, RCAF	25	Navigator
Thomas Marnoch Campbell	F/O, RCAF	21	Bomb Aimer
John Neil McDouggal	P/O, RCAF	22	Mid-Upper Gunner
Raymond Hilton Turner	P/O, RCAF	20	Rear Gunner
Mrs Lydia Helstrip	Civilian	80	28 Nunthorpe Grove
Mrs Laura Thompson	Civilian	74	28 Nunthorpe Grove
Noel Herbert Messent	Corporal	37	Pioneer Corps
Joseph Cadman	Private	35?	RAOC
Natale Giovacchini	Soldat	36	Italian PoW

Amongst the rescuers was Wing Commander Thomas E.H. Grove, a Deputy Provost Marshal in York who had seen the crash from his office in the Odeon Cinema on Blossom Street. He immediately gathered as many men and vehicles as he could before rushing to the scene. On his way to the crash site he came across the body of one of the crew in the grounds of the school some 170 yards from the main crash. The unfortunate airman had his parachute clipped on and it was partially deployed but the airman was clearly dead. Wing Commander Grove telephoned the authorities and then organised the rescuers and directed operations before being injured by an exploding bomb.

Squadron Leader James Affleck, another Deputy Provost Marshal, then established a cordon before joining the injured Wing Commander Grove in an unsuccessful attempt to extricate any surviving aircrew from the wreckage. Affleck gathered some more of his men and entered a number of houses which had been damaged and were on fire to rescue the occupants. At this point another bomb exploded and Squadron Leader Affleck was blown a considerable distance by the blast and knocked unconscious. He was carried to safety by Flight Sergeant Evans despite the fact that Evans had also suffered a serious arm injury. Upon recovering consciousness, the brave squadron leader continued to work until he was ordered to go to hospital.

Two other RAF men in the rescue party, Flight Sergeant Hodges and Sergeant Coates entered the house which was nearest to the crash site and rescued one person before they were both injured by a bomb blast. Sergeant Coates was seriously injured and taken to hospital, but Flight Sergeant Hodges insisted on resuming his rescue attempts before being ordered to hospital. Other Deputy Provost Marshals who demonstrated incredible courage were Flight Lieutenant George Larocque, Sergeant S.J. Turner and Corporal S.H.H. Blackford. Upon arrival at the scene Flight Lieutenant Larocque had been ordered to move the crowd of civilians to a safe distance before helping with rescue attempts in the shattered houses. A bomb blast left him with a splinter in his scrotum but he continued to carry out his duties despite this wound. Wing Commander Grove was awarded the George Medal, Squadron Leader Affleck the OBE, Sergeant Coates was awarded a bar to his BEM (which was gazetted in June 1945 for an earlier act of bravery), while Flight Sergeant Evans and Flight Sergeant Hodges were both awarded the BEM. Flight Lieutenant Larocque, Sergeant Turner and Corporal Blackford were all awarded the King's Commendation for Brave Conduct.

For weeks the people of York speculated on the end of the war in Europe and by the end of April 1945 the news was expected at any time. On 7 May there were widespread rumours of the German surrender and when this was confirmed that midnight on 9 May would

The Emerson crew. (Unknown)

The tail unit of the Halifax. (The Press)

be the beginning of VE-Day the people of York could rightly expect to celebrate the victory. Not everyone was in favour of such a celebration, however. Street parties did take place with dancing, music and feasting although rationing strictly limiting this). Most communities throughout Britain also celebrated by having civic buildings, war memorials and other such sites illuminated as focal points for the local community. A meeting of York council held on 8 May, however, decided by 22 votes to 19 not to illuminate any sites. The Finance Committee had recommended that 'in their opinion it would be inappropriate to have illumination or any other similar form of celebration' for VE-Day. There was considerable opposition to what seems a penny-pinching, elitist and rather miserable decision, with Councillor Ferrey arguing that principal buildings should be floodlit. She stated that failing to do so would be 'nothing short of a scandal'. Councillor Rymer agreed with her, stating that having asked the Financial Committee to organise the celebrations they had been badly let down.

Councillor Hatfield, however, supported the motion, arguing that as many York men were still engaged on the front lines against the Japanese it would be better not to celebrate until the war was completely over, while Alderman Dobbie MP also supported the motion. The MP argued that there was neither time nor manpower to fix the illuminations and made the exceptionally weak argument that it did not get dark until 11pm which meant that people would have to sit up very late to see them! The Lord Mayor explained that at the time the Finance Committee had made their decision they had not been in receipt of the government instructions allowing and encouraging both bonfires and illuminations. He went on to deliver further bad news, telling the council that due to a shortage of military bands only one was available for York and then only on one day for the Thanksgiving Day at the Minster. The Lord Mayor concluded that he was of the opinion that this was the proper day for it.

Although the authorities in York remained opposed to many forms of celebration many residents simply ignored this attitude and organised their own celebrations. Attendance at dance halls was very high and there were street parties and dances organised. Many airmen who had been fortunate enough to be given leave enlivened the scene by heading for the city but it must be said that celebrations in York were far more muted than in most other northern communities. In many streets people organised themselves and arranged bunting and flags to be flown, while

Above left: *Children celebrate VE-Day on top of an Anderson Shelter in Belle Vue Street.* (York City Council)

Above right: *Residents of York Street at their VE-Day party.* (York City Council)

Above left: *Kingsway North street party.* (York City Council)

Above right: *York children in fancy dress (one, rather oddly, as Hitler) for VE-Day.* (York City Council)

Clement Street party.
(York City Council)

*Flags and bunting in
Goodramgate on VE-Day.*
(York City Council)

others hoarded rations to gather enough food for street parties and, despite the strictures of the city council, many bonfires were lit with effigies of Hitler being particularly popular to top the fires.

With a large number of aircraft either under repair or dismantled following the surrender of Germany, the aircraft repair and dismantling yards in York were extremely busy. Many young men worked as apprentices in the yards and the experience thrilled many who felt that they had not had the chance to fly the planes as they took off on bombing operations to Germany. In June 1945 this fascination led to tragedy. George William Simpson (14) was an apprentice electrician at one such yard but was discovered dead lying beside a Halifax bomber. One of his colleagues, Edwin Coates, had gone with Simpson to the Halifax after Simpson had requested his help in removing a switch and cable. The two climbed into the bomber and noticed an odd smell. Discovering a fire extinguisher on the pilot's seat, Coates picked it up and a jet of foam shot from the extinguisher and hit Simpson in the face. Both apprentices felt dizzy and Coates left to get some fresh air. When he returned Simpson was vomiting but then insisted that he was all right. As it was nearly finishing time the two agreed to meet up that night but Coates grew worried and at 6:30pm he returned to the yard and asked after his friend. A search was organised and the body of Simpson was found next to an escape hatch on the Halifax. Simpson had vomited and a subsequent inquest recorded a verdict of accidental death due to asphyxia from methyl-bromide poisoning. The York coroner, Colonel Innes Ware, stated that Simpson had not been told to work on the bomber and advised that in the future the management should warn employees of the danger of the contents of the extinguishers.

As the Japanese forces collapsed the people of York began to look forward to the end of the war. The dropping of two atomic bombs sealed Japan's fate and it was declared that VJ-Day would be 15 August 1945 and, as had happened with VE-Day, a two-day holiday was declared. Once again the weather impacted the celebrations in York and celebrations were not as widespread as those which had greeted the end of the war with Germany. Nevertheless, many York families breathed sighs of relief as the news meant that loved ones who were fighting against the Japanese forces would return home, while those who were still serving in uniform in Britain would not now be required for service in the Far East.

CHAPTER 2

Blitz – The Air Raid of 28/29 April 1942

The final week of April 1942 began quietly with only two alarms during the afternoons of 23 and 25 April which lasted only minutes as lone enemy aircraft crossed the north-east coast at Northumberland and Wearside but no bombs were dropped. On 28 April the day had passed quietly and that night those people who were not working in York had retired peacefully to bed. Thus far, York had largely escaped the direct effects of the war. The city had experienced some 780 alerts but few bombs had dropped and there had only been four fatalities. The people of York could be excused for having grown blasé about the air raid sirens. A clear sign of this was the lack of use which the public shelters had experienced. One large shelter in the centre of the city had the key to the double-door entrance in a glass case. The first people to enter the shelter were instructed to break the glass to get the key but the glass had remained unbroken.

The people of York were probably aware that there were few sites of military importance in the city although there were some factories involved in wartime production and the nearby RAF Clifton could also have been a legitimate target. British Intelligence was aware that York was to be attacked but the city was left largely defenceless and it was over an hour before a lone RAF night fighter arrived on the scene. The Royal Observer Corps detected a large force of bombers some 30 miles off the North-East coast and saw them suddenly turn west and split into two groups which made landfall over Flamborough Head and Hornsea. The enemy aircraft were flying singly or in pairs and at altitudes ranging from 4,000 to 12,000 feet by the time they reached their target.

Unbeknownst to the people of York this was the latest in the so-called Baedeker Raids. These raids, which were in revenge for attacks on historic German towns and cities, focused on places with historic significance and a large number of heritage sites regardless of military value. The raids were characterised by the large number of incendiary bombs that were dropped.

In York the first warning of the raid was the sound of engines followed by the night being illuminated as approximately forty flares were dropped over the west of the city. Then came the explosions of the first bombs to be dropped. Ten minutes later, at 2:42am, the sirens began to wail. The first bombs were largely incendiaries which fell on Bootham Cresecent, Bootham Square, Pickering Terrace, Queen Anne's Road, and Burton Stone Lane. At the latter, a large number of soldiers from the nearby Lumley Barracks turned out to help with the fire-fighting efforts. Indeed, the early stages of the raid saw many people assisting the fire brigade and the ARP services. At Queen Anne's Road the most serious incident was at the Wellyn House Flats which were badly hit and quickly ablaze; they eventually burnt out and collapsed.

At Bootham Crescent, the National Fire Service had turned out to extinguish a fire caused by these early incendiaries but as they were working, assisted by civilians, a stick of high-explosive bombs fell on the street. The bombs straddled the railway bridge which linked Bootham Crescent and Grosvenor Terrace and resulted in the deaths of eleven people including a deputy head warden, an NFS fireman and two firewatchers. Minutes later bombs also fell on Amberley Street and at the junction of Chatsworth Terrace and Winchester Road. Those which fell on Amberley Street caused a great deal of destruction and resulted in fourteen deaths, including five members of the Button family. At Chatsworth Terrace a bomb fell just 25 yards from a group of three wardens. Two of the men were killed, the third was left in a state of severe shock and six civilians were also killed. At Queen Anne's Road seven people were killed and the local school was hit, while at 6 Pickering Terrace three people lost their lives. In Burton Stone Lane and nearby Clifton more than twenty people were trapped in the ruins of collapsed buildings and at the first location five people died.

The initial bombing led to a severe state of confusion as large numbers of reports flooded into the inexperienced ARP organisation. Many of the reports were of collapsed buildings and stated that numerous people were trapped in the rubble which necessitated the dispatch of rescue squads in addition to firefighters and wardens.

Bootham Square and Bootham Terrace were also hit. At the former 71-year-old Ellen Littlewood was killed. In Bootham Terrace several houses were destroyed but the people pulled together to provide aid to neighbours. One house became a stand-in first-aid post where shocked and injured residents gathered. Two old ladies had been killed by blast and brought to the house, it was later commented upon that they had no physical marks on their bodies. The body of a man who had also been killed by blast as he lay down to take cover was also brought in upon a door used as a makeshift stretcher.

The small street named Crossland Road, off Grant Avenue, was also hit and nos. 8 and 9 were demolished when a bomb exploded in the back yard between the two properties. The occupants of no.9, a mother and her two children, had taken cover in their Anderson shelter and were unhurt but the residents of the neighbouring property were not so fortunate. They had not taken shelter and were left buried in the rubble of their former home. Rescue workers managed to extricate a young WAAF who was relatively uninjured, followed by an injured woman and her 2-year-old son, Michael Smith, who was dead.

The most important military target in York was the railway system. The city had extensive goods and passenger lines along with sidings and repair yards and it was also home to the HQ of the London North Eastern Railway (LNER). The start of the raid coincided with the arrival of the express train from London to York. At 2:53am the express pulled into the station at platform 9. At the same time a bomb fell upon the coal depot at Leeman Road and blew rails and other debris from the sidings across the passenger lines. Fire and high-explosive bombs hitting the coal depot and stables caused massive damage. Thirty trucks were destroyed completely at the depot and the A4 Pacific Class locomotive the 'Sir Ralph Wedgewood' (No. 4469) was destroyed. The repair shed was also badly hit. At the time there were some thirty locomotives in the shed. Three of them took the brunt of the explosion and were destroyed or badly damaged, but the remainder were sheltered from the blast by these three.

The bombing in this vicinity, consisting of Leeman Road, Garfield Terrace and surrounding streets, was particularly heavy and one witness who lived in Leeman Road later reported counting eleven high-explosive bombs going off within 300 yards of his house. At the same time witnesses saw flares above the station and these were quickly followed by a number of accurately aimed high-explosive bombs and a shower of incendiaries. Several of these hit the train and wrecked it. As well as the train being wrecked, some offices were demolished and the roof was set alight. At the southern end of the station the bombs had wrecked the ticket office and set a section of the roof on fire. By this point the roof had suffered very severe damage and a large number of the offices had been wrecked. Initial firefighting efforts by station personnel and naval personnel who had been on board the express were quickly overwhelmed by the sheer number of fires in the station.

As station workers and civilians kicked incendiary bombs off the platform onto the tracks and dealt with casualties from the train, the station firemen found that the water hydrant pressure had fallen and were forced to prioritise the blazes which they made an effort to contain. As the firefighting efforts went on railway staff managed to divide the train. Six of the carriages were on fire or severely damaged and were left to burn out but fourteen were salvaged. At 4am the NFS eventually arrived on the scene, having been caught up with other incidents, and managed to run lines down to the river. Even so, it took the combined efforts of all the firemen and a further five hours to extinguish the blazes. Rumours quickly spread around the city with many uninformed

Roofless Station after the raid. (Northern Echo)

The locomotive Sir Ralph Wedgwood after being hit during the raid. (The Press, York)

witnesses, unaware of the drop in water pressure, keen to blame the efforts of the firemen for letting some fires run through the station.

The other main military target was RAF Clifton, home of the Westland Lysanders of 4 (Army Co-operation) Squadron. Bombs fell widely on the airfield and the guard room and the officers' mess were both badly damaged in the attack. The men in the guard room were reportedly all killed. Fatalities stood at seven airmen while a member of 5 Bomb Disposal Squadron, Flying Officer Ievers, was killed later in the morning while carrying out a reconnaissance of the site of two unexploded bombs which lay between Green Lane and Shipton Road.

RAF Casualties of Raid on York, 29 April 1942

Rank	Name
LAC	Frank William Gouge Barrett (31)
LAC	Ronald John Cook
LAC	George Arthur Cornell (28)
AC1	Bernard Hawcroft (20)
AC2	Harold Holmes (21)
AC2	Frank Palfreyman (19)
AC1	Charles William Shufflebotham (34)
F/O	Eyre Osbourne Ievers (38)

At the Bar Convent School on Nunnery Lane a bomb hit the premises but failed to explode. The nuns and almost thirty of their students took cover in the cellar but a roll-call revealed that one of the sisters was unaccounted for. Two of the nuns quickly went off in search of their missing companion. They were returning and were just nearing the cellar when the bomb exploded. Five nuns: Mother Mary Agnes (Madeline Clayton aged 50); Mother Mary Vincent (Eva Jordan aged 53); and Jane McClorry aged 65, Margaret Murphy aged 50, and Mary Ann O'Connor aged 39, who were all serving as firewatchers, were killed in the explosion and resulting collapse of part of the premises (their bodies were not recovered until 3 May).

The convent school was not the only educational property to be hit. Manor Grade High School was completely destroyed while Poppleton Road School also suffered a direct hit. Bootham, Nunthorpe, Queen Anne's, Shipton Street, and St Peter's schools were all damaged and several were ablaze. At King's Manor the Blind School and the neighbouring Art Gallery were also set on fire, as were the offices of the Education Department at St Leonard's and several other government offices in Dunscombe Place.

Damage at the Bar Convent. (York Libraries and Archives)

In the area of Coney Street, New Street, Daveygate and the Leopold Arcade, bombs caused extensive property damage. Amongst the buildings set on fire were the Guildhall, the church of St Martin le Grand and the neighbouring Jersey Dairy. Firefighting efforts, largely involving firemen from Malton, were quickly overwhelmed by the number of blazes in the area and by the drop in water pressure that had affected efforts at the station. At St Martin le Grand the verger dashed into the blazing building and managed to rescue the registers. Incendiary bombs caused a great deal of damage; in the grounds of a nursing home just yards from York Minster an entire cannister of incendiaries fell.

Immediately prior to the war Deathwatch beetle had been found at the Guildhall and restoration work had been ongoing for three years. The work was nearing completion at the time of the raid. Large numbers of incendiary bombs fell onto the wooden roof of the building and firefighting efforts failed to check the blazes. The magnificent Guildhall was thus completely destroyed. Aside from the heritage loss this caused significant problems to the ARP services as the Guildhall was also host to the Civil Defence Control Centre. The staff of the

St Martin le Grand Church after the Raid. (York City Archives)

control centre were horrified to learn that the secondary, emergency, control centre in St Paul's Church had also been hit and was ablaze. As a result, the control centre staff took up residence in the Mansion House and attempted to relay orders via a field telephone which was set up by the Army. The loss of command and control facilities could have been very serious indeed but the local offices of the ARP and civil defence services immediately took the initiative and were aided by the small number of bombers involved in the raid. If there had been more aircraft then it is likely that a very serious situation might have developed due to the dislocation of ARP and firefighting services.

One of the most serious fires occurred at the North Street factory owned by Rowntrees. The factory was hit early in the raid and the fire quickly took hold as the factory contained a large quantity of sugar which burned fiercely throughout the raid and into the next day.

We have already heard how lessening water pressure had affected firefighting efforts at several locations but, aside from these isolated incidents, York's firefighting organisations managed to cope reasonably well, although there was some lack of cohesion in the latter stages. They were aided in this by the fact that water could be drawn off from the Rivers Ouse and Foss while the city could also boast of no fewer than thirty-three static water tanks and the fact that 75 per cent of its planned surface water lines were already in place by this stage of the war. The number of fires did affect the pressure and firefighting efforts were aided by the use of fire boat pumps, relay lines and water from the static supplies. A greater problem was the disruption caused by the damage to telephone lines. This meant that in many cases firefighters were delayed in arriving at incidents allowing fires to get a hold and rage out of control. In many cases fires had to be left to burn. Many of these involved fires in private houses and the firefighters faced tough decisions, but fires in priority locations had to come first. During the main part of the bombing the firefighters of York were on their own, but calls for assistance were

York Guildhall ablaze during the raid. (Public Domain)

made and firefighters from several other towns and cities arrived later
on. The first such was a detachment from Hull which arrived at 4am.
This first arrival was especially fortunate and was a fine reflection
on the initiative of the NFS Area Force Commander from Hull who
had not received any request, but had grown concerned after he lost
contact with York.

Dr William Temple had been confirmed as the new Archbishop of
Canterbury just twelve days before the raid on York. Dr Temple had
been Archbishop of York since 1929 and was therefore very well
known in the city, although not always appreciated due to his stance
on the Allied bombing campaign. At the time of the raid Dr Temple
and his wife were still in York and news later surfaced of his actions
during the raid. A Scottish nursing sister, Mrs Gertrude Clouston, was
a member of the York Mobile No.1 First Aid Unit, as deputy sister

and driver. The unit had been at readiness but during the raid it was machine-gunned by a German bomber and the telephone and fuel connections were cut in addition to the windows of the first aid post being smashed. Many of the staff were taken off duty for treatment for shock.

Shortly after this Sister Clouston received the news that the post was to prepare to receive casualties. She immediately ran out into the street to find help and asked a nearby woman if she had a cycle on which she could go for help. The woman replied that she did not but that her husband would deliver her message in his car. Sister Coulston quickly scribbled down her message and handed it to the man who was introduced to her as 'My husband, the Archbishop of Canterbury'.[1] Dr Temple delivered the message successfully and then returned to the station, reported to Sister Coulston, and then went into the kitchen where he spoke with soldiers and rescue workers who were recuperating from their efforts and having a cup of tea.

In the Nunthorpe Road area several bombs fell and there were a number of casualties as well as substantial property damage in the residential streets. The Nunthorpe Estate had been constructed on land which had formerly consisted of allotments and a pond. The ground was often waterlogged and was unsuitable for the erection of Anderson shelters. One bomb dropped on nos. 19-21 Nunthorpe Grove. Typically, no.19 had no shelter and the house was demolished. At the time the house was occupied by four people, including a man who was away on night-shift, a young woman and their 3-year-old daughter. Workers frantically scoured the wreckage for survivors. The young woman was pulled from the debris and was clearly badly injured. She had suffered multiple injuries including a compound fracture of the skull and it was believed at first that even if she did survive she would have suffered irreversible brain damage. Thankfully, she went on to make a full recovery. The young girl was then discovered and pulled out. Her rescuer initially thought that the 3-year-old was dead (it was not until 42 years later that he discovered that the child had survived and had later emigrated to the USA where she married a surgeon). The fourth resident of no.19 was an ATS girl who had been billeted with the family. She was also buried and suffered two badly broken ankles. She later had an operation in which thirteen pieces of bone were removed from her left ankle.

Dr William Temple, Archbishop of Canterbury. (Public Domain)

No. 21 Nunthorpe Grove was also destroyed by the blast and the residents reported how they had been machine-gunned both before and after the bomb exploded. Only one person was missing from the property, ATS Private Dorothy Thompson who was billeted there. Dorothy was a 24-year-old from Harrogate. Investigations by members of her unit failed to find her and in the days following the raid several rescue parties searched the wreckage in vain. Inquiries at local mortuaries found that a Dorothy Thompson had been registered as having been killed on the night of the raid at the nearby village of Flaxton but this proved to be a 52-year-old local woman. By 7 May the bomb crater had become filled with water and before it could be filled in the rescue services had to borrow a pump from the NFS to pump out the water. At the bottom of the crater was a body, it was that of the unfortunate and recently engaged Dorothy Thompson.

Another bomb destroyed nos. 23-25 but without serious casualties. A further bomb exploded at the rear of the street between nos. 35-37 and 39-41. These properties were lucky enough to have Anderson shelters and there were no serious injuries even though the shelter at no.41 had its roof blown off. At the rear of Nunthorpe Grove was Nunthorpe Crescent and a number of the houses here suffered damage as a result of the blasts which impacted the neighbouring street. No.26 had a boulder thrown up from the explosion at nos. 39-41 Nunthorpe Grove crash through its roof. Mr Tom Holliday (52) was killed here but his wife was left unhurt but shocked while their daughter was rescued, suffering from back and leg injuries.

By the latter stages of the raid the civil defence services were becoming overwhelmed by the sheer number of reports of bombs and casualties which were coming in. Amongst these reports were those which stated that nearly every street from Kingsway, through Crombie Avenue, along the terraces which stood alongside the railway line as far as Grosvenor Terrace and through Bootham had been hit. In most streets there had been fatalities, while others were still unaccounted for and believed to be trapped. In the Clifton and Burton Stone Lane area approximately a score of people were trapped. Rescue workers, official and unofficial, worked feverishly to save them. Amongst the most dangerous of these tasks was that faced by those who worked to rescue a soldier and a woman who were trapped by smouldering debris near to a bomb crater. The rescue effort went on despite the danger of explosion from a nearby ruptured gas main. After two hours the two were freed successfully. There were chaotic scenes at the back of the Clifton theatre where rescuers dug through what was described as a mountain of rubble. Seven hours later a woman and a baby were rescued alive from the site.

By 4:46am the raid was over although rescue work went on. Members of the Royal Observer Corps had been witness to the entire raid from their secret post located at the sorting shed of the Central Post Office at Lendel. In the hours and days following the raid various assessments were made. It was generally believed that the ARP and civil defence services in the city had coped as well as could be expected given the nature of the raid. Particularly praiseworthy were the efforts of the civilians and service personnel who aided the services. This had been the most accurate of the Baedeker Raids with an estimated 54 per cent of all bombs landing on the target city. Fatalities of the raid have been

Bomb crater in Westminster Road. (Yorkshire Post)

Clearing the ruins. (Yorkshire Post)

put at between 76-82; 92 people were seriously injured and a further 113 injured less seriously. Damage to property was considerable with 579 houses being made uninhabitable, while a further 2,500 were damaged.

One area of considerable criticism and consternation was that of defence of the city. York had several searchlight batteries but the city, like many which were seen as being militarily unimportant, was undefended by either anti-aircraft guns or barrage balloons. The RAF night fighter response also left a lot to be desired. Only one German aircraft was claimed by an RAF fighter. Free French pilot Warrant Officer Yves Mahe (23) found himself over York during the latter stages

Bomb damage on Blake Street following the raid. (The Press, York)

of the raid and attacked several bombers. One, a Junker Ju88 crashed as it attempted to make a forced landing near Elvington.[2]

Although York was surrounded by airfields, the majority of these were Bomber Command controlled sites and the only dedicated night fighters based close to the city were those of 406 'Lynx' (RCAF) Squadron. At the time of the raid there were only four of the squadron's Bristol Beaufighters present at RAF Scorton as the squadron was not fully operational and did not formally move to Scorton until six weeks after the raid.

Casualties of the Baedeker Raid

Name	Age	Location	Notes
Adams, Thomas Cyril	37	16 Bootham Crescent	
Atkins, Ernest	45	26 Bootham Crescent	Firewatcher
Blenkin, Pauline Mary	14	39 Bootham Crescent	
Blenkin, Christine Elizabeth	11	39 Bootham Crescent	
Broadhead, Arthur	31	Bootham Crescent	NFS Fireman
Colman, George Harold	56	19 Bootham Crescent	Deputy Chief Warden
Hooker, Ada Fanny	55	30 Bootham Crescent	
Little, Florence	59	39 Bootham Crescent	
Littlewood, Ellen	71	14 Bootham Square	
MacMillan, Mary Isabel	21	16 Bootham Crescent	
Ord, Halbert	66	55 Bootham Crescent	Firewatcher
Button, James William	39	35 Amberley Street	
Button, Elsie	35	35 Amberley Street	
Button, Kenneth Ingham	15	35 Amberley Street	
Button, Audrey	12	35 Amberley Street	
Button, Gillian Patricia	1	35 Amberley Street	
Dickens, William Thomas	69	39 Amberley Street	

Name	Age	Location	Notes
Dickens, Emma	65	39 Amberley Street	
Dickens, Gertrude	40	39 Amberley Street	
Jackson, Annie	45	35 Amberley Street	
Jackson, Ella	21	35 Amberley Street	
Loveley, William Edward	68	37 Amberley Street	
Loveley, Emma	66	37 Amberley Street	
Nutter, Lola	21	35 Amberley Street	
Nutter, Kenneth Ellis	2	35 Amberley Street	
Cammidge, Lilian	51	55 Chatsworth Terrace	
Emmerson, Albert	29	Chatsworth Terrace	Air Raid Warden
Ezard, James	50	53 Chatsworth Terrace	
Ezard, Ellen Elizabeth	44	53 Chatsworth Terrace	
Ezard, Muriel	9	53 Chatsworth Terrace	
Farrington, Ada	73	14 Chatsworth Terrace	
Farrington, Sylvan	50	14 Chatsworth Terrace	
Farrow, Mary Jane	66	55 Chatsworth Terrace	
Fowler, John Herbert	34	Chatsworth Terrace	Air Raid Warden

The raid had caused such disruption that it took some time to fully assess the damage and to count the casualties and by the end of the next day the authorities could still not release the full casualty list. The local authorities in York were, however, aggrieved with the BBC and with the

Ministry of Information (MoI) after a BBC broadcast which stated that York Minster had been left undamaged by the raid. Many within the city expressed the view that this information should not have been disclosed as it might encourage further attacks by the Luftwaffe. The city council agreed with this assessment and the Lord Mayor (Mrs E.A. Crichton) wrote a letter of complaint to the Minister of Information (Brendan Bracken) which was endorsed by the Dean of York who, in an understated manner, described the BBC broadcast as indiscreet.

Despite the fact that final tallies had not been completed the authorities had made a good start on assessment and repair of the damage which had been inflicted. Many of the commercial properties had either been made good or demolition carried out, but the damage in residential areas was more problematic and in several locations was held up by the probability that trapped survivors or remains had not yet been recovered. The rescue services, assisted by volunteers, police and service personnel, worked throughout the day at such locations and several survivors were pulled alive from the wreckage.

In response to the large numbers of people who had either been left homeless or whose homes had suffered damage, the Lord Mayor immediately set up a relief fund while a special prayer service was held at the Minster for those stricken during the raid and thanks given for the sparing of much of the population. A similar service was also held in the King's Own Yorkshire Light Infantry Memorial Chapel.

The raid, however, had a transformative effect upon the city. While the mood was described as cheerful and brave a reporter from the *Yorkshire Post* reported that he had seen women who just days previously had been looking at dresses in shop windows were now to be seen in uniform wearing tin hats as they went about their duties as volunteer members of the ARP services. The reporter claimed that sights such as these added an atmosphere of dignity to the city and broadcast a spirit of resolution.

The results of the raid, however, were everywhere to be seen. Smoke still hung over many parts of the city while some streets had had glass driven into the tarmac roads and at the station the twisted girders which were hanging dangerously initially attracted many sightseers. By midday, however, the novelty of this had worn off and the crowds which had formed to gaze at the scene had dispersed and an attitude of business as usual had taken over. Indeed, the prevailing impression was of a city which had been damaged but whose spirit was unimpaired. This spirit was rallied in part by the activities of the Lord Mayor who had worked tirelessly since the raid. Mrs Crichton had worked continuously for some eighteen hours and had been sighted in every part of the stricken city. By a strange quirk of fate the Princess Royal had been due to visit York on the final day of April and it was felt important that the visit go ahead as scheduled. The Princess visited the York County Hospital where she spoke to survivors and she then toured the city, inspecting several damaged sites.

CHAPTER 3

Military Service

Women had been of vital service in the First World War and many once again quickly volunteered their services in this war. Some of the more well-established organisations were quickest off the mark but there was often some competition between them. When the First Aid Nursing Yeomanry (FANY) agreed to loan some 1,500 members to the Auxiliary Territorial Service (ATS) to act as motor mechanics it was agreed that the FANYs would remain independent of the ATS structure. The deal was reneged on, however, and the FANY/ATS members were absorbed into the latter group, although a small victory meant that they could continue to wear the FANY flash on their uniforms and the chinstrap on the top of their steel helmets. York, as headquarters of Northern Command, had a large number of female organisations with headquarters in the city. Amongst them were the Women's Voluntary Service (WVS), the ATS and the FANY. Many of the volunteers, especially those who were officers of these organisations, were themselves relatives of serving or retired members of the military.

Thus, the company commander of the 4th ATS Yorkshire Clerical Company, A.M. Masters, was the daughter of Colonel A.G. Masters (retired) and the Company Assistant, K.B. Hart-Cox, was the daughter of Colonel Hart-Cox, the Regimental Paymaster of Northern Command. Another notable member serving in the company was Senior Leader Johnston who was formerly Lady Warden of Rhodes University in South Africa.

The ladies of the WVS had an extremely active civil defence branch in York and the volunteers organised and oversaw many varying duties throughout the city. These included the running of canteens, the supervision of billets for those who had lost their homes or were evacuated to the city and a myriad of other duties. Mrs Thompson was the centre leader and she was assisted by a deputy leader (Mrs Kenny), training officer (Mrs McLellan), evacuation and canteen officer (Miss Helen Swift), transport officer (Mrs O'Callaghan), and enrolment officer (Mrs Dickinson). One of the most important branches in the working of the York WVS was the telephone exchange which had to cope with several hundred calls every day. This vital service was run by just three women (Mrs H.N. Hindley, Mrs K.B. Farrow and Miss Joyce Bell).

In York a section of FANYs who were amongst those absorbed by the ATS worked with 3rd ATS Northern Motor Company. Most were qualified motor-mechanics and were under the command of Company Commander C.M. Cowen, assisted by a number of other officers.

The disastrous Norwegian Campaign which resulted in ignominious retreat and evacuation meant the families of many York soldiers being left in anxiety over the fate of loved ones. The 1st Battalion of the York and Lancaster Regiment had been part of the campaign and

 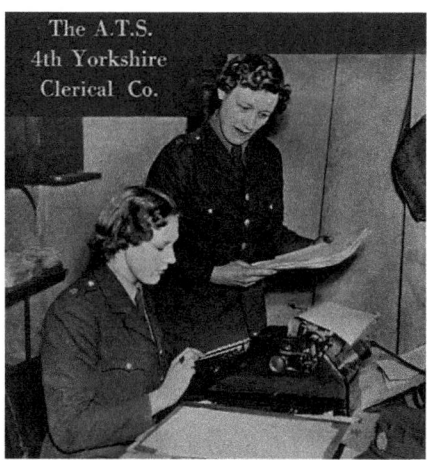

Above left: *Company Commander Masters (seated) and Company Assistant Hart-Cox, ATS.* (The Bystander)

Above right: *Senior Leader Johnston (standing) and Volunteer Olive Barton, ATS.* (The Bystander)

Right: *Sub-Leader Jose Bridgen, ATS, in charge of the Lands Branch.* (The Bystander)

Below: *WVS leaders at York. (l-r) Mrs McLellan, Miss Swift, Mrs O'Callaghan, Mrs Thompson, Mrs Kenny and Mrs Dickinson.* (The Bystander)

Above left: *York WVS telephone exchange. (l-r) Mrs Hindley, Mrs Farrow and Miss Bell.* (The Bystander)

Above right: *FANY/ATS leadership at York. Sub-Leader Clerk B.E. Kingston presents some paperwork to Company Commander R.M. Cowen.* (The Bystander)

FANY/ATS at York. (l-r) Company Assistant R.K. Thompson, Senior Leader E. Ayre, and Section Leader H. Cathcart. (The Bystander)

the fates of some of the local men who were serving were at first unknown. For some families the news of a loved one was revealed relatively speedily. Private Henry Sellars, for example, had been posted as missing at the end of April but by 23 May his anxious wife had received the news that he had been taken prisoner. Private Sellars had been in the Army for seven years, almost all of it spent in the Near East, and had just left the Army shortly before the war began. Immediately recalled, he had been in France with his battalion before they were sent to Norway.

As the Allied forces attempted to extricate themselves from the Norwegian campaign there was very fierce fighting. Some of the worst combat was around the village of Kvam where men of the 1st King's Own Yorkshire Light Infantry and 1st York and Lancaster Regiment held positions astride the main Oslo-Trondheim road. From 24-28 April the men held out against ferocious enemy attacks from land and air. Many were killed before they eventually received orders to pull back. Those who were killed in the last weeks of April were buried in a communal grave in Kvam churchyard. Amongst them was a 27-year-old soldier from the 1st Battalion King's Own Yorkshire Light Infantry who had married a York woman. Private Albert Gordon Mason was a native of Walsall and lived in Wolverhampton but had married Hilda, who was from Buchells, York.

In the days following the German invasion of France and the Low Countries it quickly became clear that Belgium and Holland would fall to the enemy. This presented several strategic problems for the British. As a result, the British landed a force in Holland in May 1940 tasked with destroying oil reserves and facilities at Rotterdam to prevent them falling into German hands. By mid-May the force, which had been landed to provide protection, was stranded and were subsequently evacuated from the Hook of Holland by a dozen destroyers of the Royal Navy. German aerial forces vigorously opposed the evacuation (Operation Ordnance) and the old destroyer HMS *Wivern* was damaged after being hit by two bombs. The bombs killed an officer and twenty-five ratings as well as injuring thirty-two others. Amongst the wounded was Petty Officer Stoker Reginald Joseph Mortimer, a married man from York who died of his wounds two days later as *Wivern* headed home. His body was brought ashore when *Wivern* reached England and he was buried at Shorncliffe Military Cemetery.

With the German Army quickly overcoming French resistance the situation in France was becoming untenable. The fighting was fierce on the land, air and sea and the men of the RAF found themselves facing fearsome odds. The vast majority of airmen who were in action during this period were pre-war regulars and the dangers of operating against a force which outnumbered them and which was often equipped with superior machines meant that the casualty rate was horrific. Among the squadrons which were forced into operating with aircraft which were obsolescent and unsuited to the roles which they were undertaking was 48 Squadron, based at RAF Detling as part of RAF Coastal Command. Operating in the maritime patrol and bombing theatre, the squadron was forced to use the Avro Ansons against what were often heavily

HMS Wivern. (Public Domain)

defended targets. On the afternoon of 20 May three Ansons were ordered to attack a number of E-boats which had been spotted off Texel. Leading the formation was a York airman who had already established himself firmly in the squadron, having served with it since January 1936. Flight Lieutenant Stephen Dodds was the 24-year-old son of Percy and Mabel Dodds and had been commissioned in the RAF as a pilot officer on 15 March 1935. Dodds took off from Detling at 5:10pm aboard Anson I (K8722, OY-G). The three aircraft sighted a convoy of eight or nine E-boats and made their attack. During his bombing run Dodds' Anson was hit in the starboard wing by flak and forced to ditch in the sea. All of the four crew were lost. Flight Lieutenant Dodds was posthumously mentioned in dispatches in the New Year's honours list on 1 January 1941.[1]

The area around Merville saw very heavy fighting as the vastly outnumbered BEF retreated in the face of the German advance. Units were often forced to reassign men to different duties during this time and one of the most important duties a soldier could undertake was in an anti-tank unit. Fusilier Arthur Eckersley was another soldier who was not a native of York (he was from Manchester) but had married a York woman. Eckersley was serving with the Royal Welch Fusiliers and had been attached to the battalion's anti-tank company when he was killed in action on 27 May, aged 36.[2]

As the men of the BEF awaited evacuation from the beaches of Dunkirk some continued to fight on, trying to hold off the German forces so that as many men as possible could be evacuated back to Britain. The seaside village of De Panne was used as the final general headquarters of the BEF from 27 May 1940. The Germans fiercely attempted to take the village and it eventually fell on the morning of 1 June. After the remaining BEF had been evacuated the Germans continued to use De Panne as the location for a military cemetery. Many of the men buried here fell in the defence of the beaches or were killed on the beaches themselves, while others were brought to the cemetery after being retrieved from the sea. One such man was York-born Private

Alec Benson of the 1st King's Own Scottish Borderers. The battalion was evacuated from the beaches on 31 May/1 June and the 25-year-old's body was later recovered from the sea indicating that he met his death while being evacuated. The chaos of the fighting in France resulted in much confusion and the fate of Private Benson was typical of this as he had initially been recorded as missing in action on 10 May before being recorded as having been killed on 28 May. Subsequently his date of death was simply recorded as having occurred between 28 May and 4 June 1940. Private Benson was a married man who left behind his wife, Irene, and his parents John and Bertha in York.

For many who knew their sons or husbands were serving with the BEF the time of the Dunkirk evacuation was one of extreme tension as they awaited news. Although many received the welcome news that loved ones had been safely evacuated and were back in Britain, others received the telegram which was dreaded by every wartime family confirming that a family member had lost their life. In the confusion of the BEF's retreat and the subsequent evacuation from the beaches it could take a good deal of time before a man's fate was established. Amongst the York families who received bad news was the Drake family. Florence Drake received the news that her son Private George Henry Drake (32) had been killed in action on 1 June while serving with the 1st Battalion Duke of Wellington's (West Riding Regiment). Like many who were lost during this confused campaign Private Drake has no known grave and is commemorated on the Dunkirk Memorial.

As the men of the BEF returned home to Britain their stories began to emerge. Many of these were, of course, filtered through the censored and patriotic lens of the media. On 3 June 1940, for example, the *Yorkshire Post & Leeds Intelligencer* ran an article in which several Yorkshire soldiers related their experiences. One soldier explained how he had always thought that the stories of German atrocities had been propaganda until he had seen German aircraft machine-gunning roads packed with refugees, including small children. He gave his opinion that, because 'Jerry doesn't fight clean', Britain should take 'off the gloves to him' and fight the German 'in the only manner he understands'. Another soldier added that the RAF had done magnificently and that with more aircraft they would have defeated the Germans, adding that on one occasion at Dunkirk he had witnessed two Spitfires chasing a dozen German bombers.

As the Battle of Britain raged a motor accident claimed the life of a York soldier who had celebrated his marriage a fortnight previously. Lance Corporal Arthur Vincent Leadley had worked in the York offices of the West Yorkshire Road Car Company before joining the Army in April 1940. He had married a former co-worker at the company and it was at her home in Keighley that his wife received the tragic news on 28 July 1940.

The Norway campaign continued to make headlines as the fates of men who had been reported missing were gradually revealed. Several regiments with strong Yorkshire connections had been involved in the fighting, including the King's Own Yorkshire Light Infantry, the York and Lancaster Regiment, and the Green Howards. On 9 August 1940 the *Yorkshire Post & Leeds Intelligencer* reported that a group of 125 men had been repatriated from neutral Sweden. Two of the men from the York and Lancaster Regiment, Sergeant G.S.W. Frank and Company Sergeant Major (CSM) John T. McCarthy, recounted their experiences to the newspaper. Although they attempted to portray the pluckiness of the British forces and stuck to what was obviously an official line, their experiences clearly showed the confusion and chaos which had marked the campaign and doomed it to failure. CSM McCarthy explained how he had been told that around 4,000 Germans were also being interned by Sweden, including 'between three and four hundred of the enemy's best airmen'. This was completely untrue but was obviously intended to bolster home morale and to imply that the fighting had not all been one-sided. Sergeant Frank explained how he had been involved in the fighting at Sjoa after his unit had been landed at Molde. He described how the British had faced off a superior number of enemy soldiers but that the German assault had in the end forced them to withdraw. Once again there was an attempt to portray the British efforts in a good light when Sergeant Frank assured the reporter that, before being forced to withdraw, his unit had made a 'fairly successful counter-attack, in which headquarters staff, batmen and cooks were engaged'.[3] Clearly, however, the counter-attack had not been successful at all as they had later been force to withdraw. The fact that it had proved necessary to make the attack using men who were generally non-combatant demonstrated the desperation of the British in this action. Sergeant Frank went on to describe how his unit had been forced to disperse into small groups and had moved through the snow-shrouded countryside for several days and nights as they tried to avoid capture. The men in his group had experienced severe hardship and been forced to shelter in mountain caves and outhouses. At one point they had been without food for five days and had been forced to drink melted snow when their water supply ran out. Several men grew ill or too tired to continue as their position grew more and more hopeless and were left behind. Sergeant Frank himself had been taken ill and was forced to rest, however the sergeant was fortunate and was taken in by a Norwegian farmer who looked after him for a month. When he had recovered sufficiently, he was given civilian clothing and a week's supply of food and he set off for Narvik where he hoped to link up with British forces. After learning that the British had evacuated Narvik he made for the Swedish border.

With a German invasion considered likely the attempt to disrupt German shipping and enemy held ports continued apace throughout August. Amongst the units which had been thrown into this makeshift campaign was 53 Squadron which, despite a lack of training in night-flying, found itself undertaking the duty of a night bomber squadron attacking enemy ports. On the evening of 3 August several Blenheim bombers were sent to attack Emden's harbour facilities. Blenheim IV (L9475, PZ-V) failed to return. The aircraft had been detected flying out at sea off Norfolk at 12:45am but wireless communication abruptly ceased some twenty minutes later and it was believed that the aircraft had crashed into the sea. The body of the observer was washed up in France, while that of the pilot was washed up on the English coast. That of the navigator, York-born Sergeant Kenneth Walter Crane (22), was never recovered.[4]

The final day of August saw the 20th Destroyer Flotilla off the Dutch island of Texel. The flotilla had been ordered to lay a minefield to harass enemy shipping. Amongst the destroyers was HMS *Esk*, an E-Class destroyer which had been built so as to be rapidly converted to duty as a fast minelaying vessel. While laying mines an enemy force was detected and the flotilla moved to intercept but ran into an undetected minefield. HMS *Express* had her bow blown off and the flotilla commander aboard HMS *Esk* moved to her aid only to strike a mine. The destroyer sank very quickly and there was only one survivor. Amongst the dead was Able Seaman Charles Ernest Sunderland (22) from York.

September 1940 saw units of the Royal Navy engaged against a variety of Italian targets. On 15 September a force led by the aircraft-carrier HMS *Illustrious* and consisting in addition of the battleship HMS *Valiant*, heavy cruiser HMS *Kent*, anti-aircraft cruisers HMS *Calcutta* and *Coventry* and seven destroyers left Alexandria to attack Benghazi. On 16/17 September aircraft from *Illustrious* mined the harbour of Benghazi and attacked enemy shipping. At the time *Kent* and two destroyers were detached to bombard Bardia. On the following night HMS *Kent* was attacked by Italian torpedo bombers and hit by a single torpedo on the stern. The stricken cruiser was towed back to port by an escorting destroyer. Amongst the casualties aboard the cruiser was at least one York sailor, Able Seaman Harry Martin Welsh aged 25. His body was buried at sea and he is commemorated on the Chatham Naval Memorial.

A number of York men found themselves at the front during the Battle of Britain. Malcolm Gray was born in York in January 1920 and was the only son of his parents, George and Emily. Malcolm had been educated at Archbishop Holgate's School and after leaving had begun training as an architect with a local firm. He was a sporty young man and pursued an interest in tennis, but he also was a skilled pianist and loved his Rudge 500 motorcycle. Like many young men of the time he was fascinated by flying and he joined the Royal Air Force Volunteer Reserve (RAFVR) in 1938.

Called up at the start of September 1939, he had already completed his pilot training and was quickly posted to the Spitfire-equipped 72 Squadron at RAF Leconfield on 12 September. Sergeant Gray, nicknamed 'Mabel' Gray, operated as part of the squadron throughout the spring of 1940 and when 72 Squadron was posted south in June he went with them to RAF Gravesend to support the Dunkirk evacuation. After this first combat experience the squadron was sent north once more to RAF Acklington in Northumberland. On 29 June Gray shared in the destruction of a Dornier Do18 over the Firth of Forth. At the end of August they were sent south to RAF Biggin Hill. The squadron was to relieve the badly mauled 610 Squadron and upon arriving at their new station they could have been in no doubt that they were now in the very front line. Biggin had been badly bombed on the days prior to their arrival and 72 Squadron was sent to RAF Croydon the day after their arrival in the south. Over the next three days of bitter aerial fighting 72 Squadron acquitted itself well. The squadron did not lose a single pilot, although eleven of its Spitfires were written off and others damaged during this period when they often operated from a forward base at RAF Hawkinge. Gray claimed two Do18s probably destroyed on 1 and 2 September respectively.

By the afternoon of 5 September the squadron had only nine serviceable aircraft left and these were scrambled to make an interception on a force of enemy bombers approaching Thameshaven. Unfortunately, the squadron had been scrambled too late and as they were struggling to gain height over Elham they were bounced by two formations of Me109s and Me110s. The three Spitfires at the rear of the formation were shot down. Pilot Officer Deacon-Elliott reported that he saw Sergeant Gray being very badly hit. In his opinion his comrade would have been killed instantly and he saw Gray's Spitfire 1 (N3093) dive vertically into the ground.

Observers on the ground also witnessed the last moments of this York airman. Witnesses saw an Me110 rake a Spitfire with heavy fire before pulling away. The Spitfire fell vertically but before hitting the ground it flattened out of its dive and fell in small spirals before hitting Elham Park Wood. Two brothers, Walter and William Wood, raced to the scene of the now burning Spitfire. The two bravely looked into the blazing cockpit but could see no sign of a pilot. Once the fire had almost burned out an RAF airman arrived on a motorcycle. He had already located the crash sites of the other two aircraft from 72 Squadron and told the two brothers that the pilot of this one was dead. A subsequent inspection revealed the charred remains of Malcolm Gray (20) underneath the instrument panel. Shortly after the Spitfire had burned out a photographer arrived and placed his camera only to be told that the body of the pilot was still in the cockpit. A tarpaulin was draped over the cockpit before the photograph was taken. This courageous York airman left behind not only his family but also his pregnant fiancée, Gwyneth, whom he was to marry on his next leave.[5]

After the fall of France the Royal Navy was desperate for ships and a number of former French vessels were commandeered and put to use. Amongst them was the armed merchant ship which became HMS *Listrac*. The ship was a steam coaster but was to be used as an armed auxiliary patrol vessel despite her lack of armour. On the night of 11/12 October 1940 she was patrolling the Channel in company with naval trawler HMS *Warwick Deeping* when the two came under fire from five German destroyers. The captain of the *Listrac* believed that they had mistakenly been attacked by Royal Navy ships and turned on his identification lights. As a result, the ship was quickly shelled, causing a large explosion, before being torpedoed and sunk with the loss

Sgt Malcom 'Mabel' Gray. (Public Domain)

of her captain and eleven of her crew. Amongst them was another York seaman. Lieutenant Kenneth Powell Kirkup was aged 29 and had grown up in York where he had married. Before the war he had won the Silver Medal of the Royal Humane Society.[6]

As the Royal Navy attempted to interdict German shipping the men of the submarine service took part in ever more frequent patrols. HMS *Swordfish* had already undertaken eleven wartime patrols by 7 November 1940 when she departed Portsmouth bound for the Bay of Biscay. The boat was supposed to check in on 15 and 16 November but nothing was heard and the submarine and her forty crew were assumed to have been sunk in the Bay of Biscay by either German destroyers or a mine. It was not until 1983 that the wreck of HMS *Swordfish* was discovered lying in 46 metres of water off St Catherine's Point, Isle of Wight. The submarine had been split in half just forward of her deck-gun by a mine and in all likelihood had been sunk on the very day on which she had set out. Amongst her crew was David Jameson Sproat, a York-born Stoker 1st Class aged 24.[7]

Just a month after the loss of HMS *Swordfish* another York submariner was lost. HMS *Triton* had sailed from Malta on 28 November to patrol

HMS Swordfish. (Public Domain)

the southern Adriatic Sea. It is believed she attacked and damaged an Italian merchant ship but then contact was lost. The exact fate of the boat is unknown with Italian sources claiming that she was sunk by Italian torpedo boats but the Admiralty believing that she was lost to naval mines in the Strait of Otranto. Amongst her crew was Able Seaman John Robert Day, a 30-year-old married man.[8]

Amongst the most risky professions that could be undertaken during the war was service in the Merchant Navy. Losses amongst the ships and men of the service were truly horrendous throughout the war and particularly from 1939-1943 and many York families suffered the loss of loved ones aboard merchant ships. On 2 December 1940 the motor tanker MV *Victor Ross* was steaming for America as part of Convoy OB-251 when she was hit by two torpedoes fired by *U-43*. The submarine closed in and fired a coup-de-grace, causing the tanker to sink stern first while some 355 miles from the Bloody Foreland; all 44 of the crew were lost. Amongst them was 15-year-old Mess Room Boy David Brown, the son of Wilfred and Phyllis Brown of York.[9]

The training of novice aircrew was a dangerous undertaking and in this period claimed many victims. On 22 December 1940, for example, yet another York trainee airman was lost due to an accident. Pilot Officer J.H. Dales (30) was the son of a York corn merchant and an old boy of St Peter's School, York. Before the war he had been employed in his father's business but, like many York men, he had decided to enlist in the RAF shortly after the war began. On 22 December he was stationed at RAF Upwood as part of 17 Operational Training Unit (OTU). Pilot Officer Dales had taken off aboard Bristol Blenheim IV (L4896) with Pilot Officer C.S. Romach at the controls. Little further is known except that the aircraft crashed at 11:50am close to Market Harborough after flying into high tension cables. From this it appears that the crew were either in difficulties or were indulging in some illicit low-level flying.[10]

The units of the York Home Guard took part in a large and varied number of exercises to train and hone their skills and to perfect tactics as the duties of the Home Guard continued to evolve. These exercises were always well-attended and were usually met with a high degree of enthusiasm by the men of the Home Guard. In July 1941, for example, an unspecified York Home Guard battalion took part in an exercise in which it made a highly successful night attack on a regular Army unit which was acting as an invading force. The Home Guard battalion utilised its extensive mobility and several specialised units during the exercise. It was through exercises such as these that the Home Guard developed its abilities and also earned greater appreciation as a force through its developing professionalism.

One victim of the raid mounted by RAF Bomber Command on the night of 2 September 1941 was a Halifax bomber which the Germans claimed had been shot down by anti-aircraft fire. On 5 September the German news agencies reported that at least two of the crew had baled out and had been taken prisoner. The Germans named these unlucky airmen as being Sergeant Richard Arthur from London and Sergeant Thomas Edwin Allison who was from York.

One of the most dangerous duties during the war was that of serving aboard a submarine of the Royal Navy. Not only were the conditions on such vessels extremely trying, but the chances of escaping from a submerged submarine were very slim indeed. In December 1941 HMS *Perseus* failed to return from a patrol in the Mediterranean and was declared lost. It was believed that the submarine had struck a mine on 6 December and of the sixty-one men who were aboard there was only one survivor, although this was not known until much later. Amongst those to lose their lives was yet another married York man, Steward Albert Ernest Hartley (28) who left behind his widow, Maud Marion Hartley, and his parents, Albert and Florence, in York.[11]

Large numbers of service personnel from York were in the front lines facing the enemy and while the majority of the public's attention was devoted to the war against Germany the fight against Imperial Japan concerned many in the city, especially those who had friends and relatives fighting this foe in far-flung theatres of war. In the Pacific the Japanese

HMS Perseus. (Public Domain)

forces invaded the island of Java at the end of February 1942. The Japanese quickly gained ground and the Allies (consisting of units from the UK, USA, Australia and the Netherlands) were forced to surrender on 12 March. The initial stages of the campaign, however, saw intensive naval action in which the Allies came off decidedly the worse. The main naval battle occurred on 27 February, the day before the landings, during what became known as the Battle of the Java Sea. During the battle the Allied Eastern Strike Force made repeated attempts to push through Japanese naval units in order to attack the invasion fleet. The Allies lost a heavy cruiser, two light cruisers and three destroyers and were forced to retreat.[12] With the situation appearing irredeemable the surviving naval units attempted to flee to the safety of Australia over the next few days.[13] Amongst those ships was the S-class destroyer HMS *Stronghold*. On 2 March, however, the destroyer was spotted in the Java Sea by Japanese aircraft and her position was relayed to the Imperial Japanese Navy forces. *Stronghold* was intercepted by the heavy cruiser

Maya and the destroyers *Arashi* and *Nowaki*. Despite being under fire from the cruiser's main armaments the British destroyer managed to evade the early fire, the *Maya* fired more than 600 shells, but shortly before 7pm the destroyer was hit, immobilised and on fire. Shortly afterwards it exploded and sank taking seventy-four of her crew to their deaths. Amongst the dead was Able Seaman Ernest Smith of York, a 26-year-old married man who left his widow Ethel and his parents, Albert and Lilian.[14]

The end of March 1942 saw another York sailor lose his life while serving aboard a destroyer. The Dunkirk veteran HMS *Jaguar* was part of the escort for the fleet oiler *Slavol* and in the early hours of 26 March was off Egypt when she was struck by two torpedoes fired by *U-652*. The torpedoes struck the forward section of the destroyer and she quickly caught fire and sank with the loss of three officers and 190 of her crew, while 8 officers and 45 crewmen survived to be rescued. Amongst those lost was Chief Petty Officer (CPO) Ernest Preston, a 37-year-old married man from York.[15]

On 28 March 1942 the Allies mounted Operation Chariot, an audacious attack on the dry-dock facilities at the French port of St Nazaire. The operation was a qualified success but came at a very high cost to the attacking forces. Part of the force was to be landed in motor launches and these small vessels suffered exceptionally heavy losses due to the withering enemy fire. Amongst the motor launches on the operation was HMML 192, under the command of Lieutenant Commander Bill Stevens. This was one of many motor launches to be hit and set on fire during the run in to the target and she sank with loss of many lives. HMML 192 and her sister vessel were both hit and sunk at the same time and from their complements of crew and commando passengers there were only six survivors who were all captured. Amongst the dead was Motor Mechanic George Snowball, a 20-year-old native of York who was later posthumously mentioned in dispatches for his marked courage, skill and determination displayed during the St Nazaire operation.[16]

HMS Jaguar dropping depth charges in 1940. (Public Domain)

The men of the Home Guard had often had to put up with being mocked in the immediate weeks and months after their formation as people derided them for their lack of equipment, uniforms, weapons and training. Mockingly called 'Look, Duck and Vanish' and other sarcastic epithets and scorned as being a group of older men playing at being soldiers while getting in the way, the men earned grudging respect for the roles they played during air raid alerts and in guarding facilities and therefore freeing up regular soldiers for other duties. As the force became better armed and equipped and more professional, as well as being renamed the Home Guard, attitudes changed and by 1942 the Home Guard was largely appreciated for the work it performed, despite the fact that invasion was now far less likely.

During the horrific raid of 29 April 1942 the Home Guard played a leading and important role in aiding not only the meagre defences of the city, but also in assisting the ARP and civil defence services. The individual Home Guards who were on duty were placed at great risk as they had to remain outside during the raid. One young Home Guardsman did not realise the risk he was in until many years after the raid. Aged just 17 at the time of the raid, Dennis Joseph Durkin found himself stationed on top of the York gasometer in order to spot and report any breaches of the blackout regulations. Mr Durkin later recalled that he and his comrades had heard an aircraft fly over the city at the very beginning of the raid but had assumed it was British as the air raid sirens had not sounded. It was only when a bomb dropped nearby that they realised their error. It was not until 2007 that Mr Durkin read an account in which the gasometer was described as a primary target for the raiders.[17]

The need for fuel meant that the tankers of the Merchant Navy were hugely overstretched to maintain supplies and the men and ships paid a very heavy price for their efforts with many vessels being sunk and a large number of men killed. In an effort to help protect vulnerable merchant vessels some 5,500 were designated as Defensive Equipped Merchant Ships (DEMS) and were armed and supplied with a crew of Royal Navy gunners. On 14 July 1942 the tanker SS *British Yeoman* was southwest of the Canary Islands and in dire trouble. The unescorted tanker had been hunted by a U-boat for some fourteen hours. At 1:46am on 15 July her luck ran out and she was hit by a torpedo from *U-201*. The stricken tanker immediately caught fire. The fire upon the water forced the U-boat to leave the scene but when she returned the next morning she found the stern section of the tanker still afloat and sank it with gunfire. Of the crew complement of fifty-three there were only ten survivors. Amongst the dead were seven Royal Navy gunners including 33-year-old Able Seaman William Shaw, a York man.[18]

On 8 November 1942 the Allies launched Operation Torch, the invasion of French North Africa. The operation required a very heavy naval operation to support the land forces. Amongst Force-H, which was to cover the landings at Algiers and Oran, was the destroyer HMS *Martin*. The destroyer had only been launched in 1940 (built by Vickers-Armstrong at Newcastle) but had led a very active wartime life. On 10 November, however, she was torpedoed by *U-431*. As a result of this HMS *Martin* blew up and sank with the loss of all but 64

SS British Yeoman. (Public Domain)

of her 190-man crew. Amongst the dead was yet another York sailor, Able Seaman Joseph Taylor aged 20.[19]

As the year 1943 opened RAF Bomber Command was expanding in preparation for the launch of its main offensive against Germany which would begin in March. Huge numbers of volunteers were spread across the United Kingdom training to become airmen. The path to becoming aircrew in Bomber Command was highly dangerous and a great many young volunteers lost their lives while still training. On the night of 11 January Armstrong Whitley V (LA 766) of No. 81 Operational Training Unit took off from RAF Tilstock in Shropshire on a night navigational exercise. Shortly before 9pm the Whitley crashed near Wrexham. Of the eight men on board, seven were killed outright while the eighth died on his way to hospital. Amongst the crew was 21-year-old Sergeant Michael John Buckle of York. His proud parents, Edward and Florence had the following placed upon his headstone in York Cemetery: 'ONE OF A GALLANT CREW'.

Over two consecutive nights on 16/17 and 17/18 January 1943 Bomber Command raided the German capital Berlin. On the second night a force of 187 bombers was sent but results were very poor and night fighters managed to penetrate the bomber stream and take a fearsome toll of the British aircraft; a total of twenty-two bombers were lost, some 11.8 per cent of the force. Amongst them were four Lancasters from No. 9 Squadron based at RAF Waddington. Two were confirmed as having crashed while the remaining pair disappeared without trace. Lancaster I (W4157, WS-V) had taken off at 4:58pm with Flight Sergeant T.L. Gibson, RCAF, at the controls. The Lancaster and its eight-man crew (it was carrying a second-pilot who was gaining operational experience) vanished and all of the crew were later commemorated on the Runnymede Memorial. The bomb-aimer in the crew was Sergeant Bernard Kenneth Skinner, RAF, a 28-year-old York man.

It was not only the men serving as aircrew who placed their lives at risk in the winter of 1943. Those who served as groundcrew, servicing the aircraft and loading bombs, fuels and ammunition also had an extremely dangerous role and many were killed either in accidents or through illness. On 7 February York Aircraftsman 2 Norman Ward (21) lost his life while serving as part of 51 Squadron. He and others were tragically killed in a traffic accident.[20] A large group of RAF men were returning from a night out in nearby Pontefract. The men were packed into two RAF buses but as they were passing through Knottingley the rearmost vehicle failed to negotiate a bend near to the Town Hall and crashed into the wall of a vicarage. Police, civil defence workers and members of the public raced to the scene and began the task of extricating the injured and dead from the wreckage. Only four people managed to escape injury (including the driver) aboard the bus. Three were only slightly injured and were allowed to return to RAF Snaith but five RAF men were found dead at the scene and three more died in hospital.[21]

On 14 February 1943 many a young airman must have been looking forward to a Valentine's Day tryst, but the plans of the airmen of Bomber Command were disrupted when they were briefed for operations on the night of 14/15. On this night the command was split into two with a force of 243 aircraft made up of Halifaxes, Wellingtons and Stirlings attacking Cologne while a force of 142 Lancasters attacked Milan. Amongst the crews briefed to attack Cologne was that of Sergeant L.W. Tabor, RNZAF, of No. 90 Squadron at RAF Ridgewell. Tabor and his crew took off shortly after 7pm aboard Stirling I (RF 438, WF-D) but nothing further was heard from the crew and they were declared missing. The navigator was another York airman, Sergeant Edward Couldwell (21), the son of James and Felicia Couldwell.[22]

On 2 March 1943 RAF Bomber Command made another attempt to cause serious damage to the German capital when it launched a major raid involving 302 aircraft. Although marking and bombing were scattered, the larger number of aircraft ensured that more damage was done to Berlin on this raid than on any other so far in the war. The raid cost the Command seventeen aircraft. Flying Officer N.S. Black and his No. 76 Squadron crew took off from RAF Linton-on-Ouse at 6:20pm and was last heard on wireless at 9:48pm. Flying Officer Black's flight engineer was Sergeant Herbert John Gruntman, a 23-year-old married man from York.[23]

Although the submarine service was highly successful during the war, their losses were high. HMS *Turbulent* was a T-Class submarine built at Barrow and launched in 1941 before spending most of her career in the Mediterranean. By late February 1943 HMS *Turbulent* had successfully sunk twenty-two enemy vessels and damaged several more. On 1 March she is believed to have sunk an Italian steamer and two days later she shelled and sank two Italian motorsailers. Eleven days later an Italian anti-submarine trawler reported attacking a submarine. HMS *Turbulent* failed to respond to communications and did not return to base. It was assumed that she had been sunk on 12 March but subsequent research has shown that the submarine attacked (unsuccessfully) by the trawler was a French boat and it is now suspected that HMS *Turbulent* was in fact lost on 6 March when an Italian torpedo boat reported making a depth-charge attack on a submarine south of Naples. Amongst those lost was 31-year-old York-born Engine Room Artificer 4th Class George Leonard Mason who left a widow, Annie. To add to the confusion, the CWGC continues to give the date of death as being 23 March but it is commonly accepted that the submarine was in all likelihood lost on 6 March.

On the night of 5/6 March 1943 Bomber Command launched its main offensive with a raid on Essen. From now the scale of raiding would pick up and the command was reinforced both in terms of numbers and machines with numerous squadrons re-equipping with the newer four-engine heavy bombers. No. 77 Squadron at nearby RAF Elvington was one such squadron having recently turned in its Whitleys for newer Halifax bombers. On the night of 9/10 March the command briefed 264 of its crews for a raid on the southern German city of Munich. Despite high winds heavy damage was done in parts of the city for the loss of only eight aircraft. Amongst those lost was the first No. 77 Squadron Halifax to fail to return from operations. Halifax II (JB 795, KN-H) took off shortly after 8pm with a 22-year-old York pilot at the controls. Flying Officer John Basil O'Connell Huggard and his crew were shot down and their Halifax crashed into Lake Konstanz, killing all of the crew.[24]

Attacks against Berlin continued through March and another raid, this time consisting of 329 aircraft, took place on 29/30 March. Weather conditions were bad and this contributed to very poor bombing results with most of the bombs falling in open countryside. Some twenty-one bombers failed to return. At RAF Syerston the very experienced crew of one of No. 106 Squadron's flight commanders failed to return. Squadron Leader E.L Hayward DFC and his crew had taken off in Lancaster III (ED596, ZN-H) at 9:25pm but it was shot down by a night fighter on its way home and crashed in Holland at approximately 4:30am. The crew's navigator was Flight Lieutenant John Oswald Young DFC, a 21-year-old from York.[25]

Although the majority of the air offensive was carried on by the heavy bombers, the light bombers of No. 2 Group continued to play a role making precision attacks, often against targets in occupied Europe. These raids often came at a very heavy price. On 21 April 1943, for example, eleven Lockheed Venturas of No. 21 Squadron took off to attack the railway yards at Abbéville. The formation attacked their target successfully but shortly after leaving the target area they were set upon by enemy fighters and three of the bombers were shot down with the loss of all twelve crewmen. One of the Venturas shot down was that of Flying Officer G.B. Chippendale, his wireless operator/air gunner was Pilot Officer Arthur William (Bill) Richmond, a 32-year-old married man from York. The inscription on his grave reads: IN LOVING MEMORY OF BILL BELOVED HUSBAND OF VIOLET. LOVES LAST GIFT, REMEMBRANCE.[26]

While the general public keenly followed the bombing campaign which was progressing against Germany, there was less awareness of the role which Bomber Command played in sinking and inhibiting enemy shipping through the dropping of sea mines. These operations were commonly known as 'gardening' and the mines were referred to as 'vegetables'. These sorties were often viewed as being less dangerous than operations over Germany, but the truth was that many airmen lost their lives while 'gardening'. On the nights of 27/28 and 28/29 April 1943 Bomber Command mounted 367 'gardening' sorties. On the first night only one aircraft was lost but on the second occasion the force suffered the heaviest loss of a minelaying force during the entire war with twenty-two bombers failing to return. At RAF Newmarket there was consternation in the ranks of No. 75 (New Zealand) Squadron as four of their Stirlings failed to return. One of the lost bombers was Stirling III (BF467, AA-W). The Stirling, skippered by Pilot Officer D.L. Thompson, RNZAF, was hit by flak and crashed into the Baltic shortly after midnight, killing all on board. The crew included yet another York airman. Sergeant Clifford Abbott was the 21-year-old flight engineer in Pilot Officer Thompson's crew. His parents, Joseph and Grace, lived in Clifton, York.[27]

As the men of Bomber Command continued with the Battle of the Ruhr new technology began to make an impact in the bomber war.

It was hoped that one innovation, codenamed 'Oboe', would help increase the accuracy of bombing, even in poor weather, through the use of converging radar beams. To test this development a series of smaller raids were made on towns which had rarely or never been bombed before. On the night of 14/15 June the command sent 197 Lancasters to attack Oberhausen in complete cloud. The attack was a success but seventeen of the Lancasters were lost. At RAF Dunholm Lodge No. 44 (Rhodesia) Squadron had lost two bombers. One was piloted by a flight commander but the other was flown by a 19-year-old Londoner, Sergeant Peter James Shearmen. The flight engineer in the crew was Flight Sergeant Edward Lockington Pugh, a 22-year-old native of Fulford, York.[28]

York airmen flew in every RAF command and in every conceivable theatre of war. One of the most far-flung squadrons was No. 204 Squadron which, in 1943, was flying Short Sunderland flying boats on anti-submarine operations off the coast of Africa. The Sunderland had an exceptional range and the aircraft of 204 Squadron were also used for a variety of transport tasks. On 18 July Sunderland III (JM687) was tasked with transporting a number of passengers between Gibraltar and Britain. The Sunderland was shot down and the fourteen people on board were killed. One of the crew was York air gunner, Sergeant Alfred Thompson (20).[29]

We have already seen how many York airmen lost their lives during training and yet another life was lost on 23 July when 21-year-old Sergeant Reginald Douglas Eaglen and his two comrades were killed when their Bristol Beaufort I (JM451) of 5 (C) OTU crashed in Northern Ireland. Sergeant Eaglen, a trainee wireless operator/air gunner, was a native of York although he lived in Essex at the time of his death.[30]

During the final days of July and the first days of August 1943 Bomber Command mounted four attacks on the city of Hamburg within just ten days. The battle was hugely successful and much of the port city was utterly destroyed, largely in a firestorm which swept through the city as a result of the second raid on the night of 27/28 July. Bomber losses were less than would be expected due to the first use of a device known as 'Window' which consisted of specially designed foil strips which were ejected from the bombers to disrupt enemy radar defences. On the night of the firestorm Bomber Command had sent 787 aircraft to attack Hamburg. Seventeen of these failed to return. At RAF Mildenhall No. 15 Squadron lost two of its Stirling bombers and on board one was yet another young York airman. Sergeant Ernest Edward Roberts Gomersall was the 19-year-old mid-upper air gunner in the Stirling III (EH893, LS-J) of the experienced Flight Lieutenant J.E. Childs. The Stirling had taken off shortly before 10pm but over the target had been hit by flak and as it tried to escape the target zone it was picked off by a night fighter. Only one man escaped of the eight on board but Sergeant Gomersall was killed. The young air gunner had been an accomplished sportsman at school and had been Junior Victor Ludorum at Heath Grammar School in 1933. Like many such young men he had applied for aircrew duties while still underage as a deferred service candidate and was called up in late 1941. His parents, Ernest and Amy, received the news that their son was missing at their home in Acomb.[31]

For those women who were married to men serving as aircrew in the RAF life was dominated in part by the constant fear and anxious anticipation over their husband. Due to radio broadcasts and word of mouth the civilian population were well aware that Bomber Command in particular, was paying an extremely heavy price for the almost constant raids which it was mounting against Germany. For those in York this awareness was heightened by the fact that the city lay in 'bomber country', with numerous airfields of No. 4 and 6 Groups scattered across the nearby countryside. The casualties being suffered, however, were across every RAF command.

Minnie Smitham, a young woman from York, had married a Cumbrian man, Flight Sergeant William Henry Smitham. In July 1943 the 23-year-old was a pilot serving in Coastal Command with No. 612 (County of Aberdeen) Squadron at RAF Chivenor. Designated a maritime reconnaissance squadron, it had recently re-equipped with specialised reconnaissance versions of the Vickers Wellington and, in July, was tasked largely with flying anti-submarine patrols over the Bay of Biscay. On the night of 3 August 1943 Flight Sergeant Smitham and his crew took off at 11:15pm in Wellington XIV (MP654, WL-J) but suffered engine problems and returned to base in the early hours of 4 August. The crew were quickly allocated a replacement aircraft and took off at 1:48am in Wellington XIV (HF128, WL-P). Nothing further was heard and the Wellington failed to return. As a result the whole crew were posted as missing and later confirmed as having lost their lives. For Mrs Smitham these events began a long and torturous experience as she was initially informed that her husband was missing as a result of operations. The official communiqué confirming Flight Sergeant Smitham as missing was not issued until 21 October and it was not until almost a year later on 20 July 1944 that her husband was officially confirmed as killed.

The expansion of the RAF meant that the service had a voracious appetite for new airmen. The training process was long and arduous and large numbers of newly qualified pilots who had potential found themselves posted, not as they expected to service squadrons but as instructors, others were posted as instructors after completing a tour of operation with a service squadron. Robert Peter Abbey was one such instructor. A York man, he had joined the RAF in 1940 and had been commissioned as a pilot officer on 1 May 1942 before being promoted to flying officer in November of that year. By August 1943 he was serving as a pilot instructor at No. 5 Pilot's Advanced Flying (PAFU). On 9 August 1943 he was flying a dual-training detail with a Canadian student, Sergeant H.D. Tushingham, in Miles Master II (DL609). While Flying Officer Abbey was demonstrating the procedures for a forced landing the aircraft stalled during a low turn, crashed, and caught fire near the village of Calverley. Both the student and 22-year-old Flying Officer Abbey were killed.[32]

On the night of 10/11 August 1943 Bomber Command made a major raid on the distant southern German city of Nuremburg. The attack was successful but sixteen aircraft failed to return. At RAF Graveley No. 35 Squadron of the Pathfinders had dispatched twenty-one of its Halifaxes with one failing to return. Halifax II (HR861, TL-T) had taken off at 11:36pm but nothing further was heard and the aircraft and crew were declared missing. The crew was an experienced and able one. It later emerged that the Halifax had been attacked by a night fighter over Worms and had caught fire. There was confusion aboard with surviving crew members later reporting that the fire in the fuselage made communication impossible and the bomb aimer reporting that the flight engineer had appeared dazed and that he had clipped the flight engineer's parachute on him but had not seen him bale out. The Halifax exploded shortly after it had been attacked and four of the crew (the pilot, navigator, bomb aimer and wireless operator) managed to escape but the remaining three men were killed. Sergeant Jackett and his two comrades are buried at Rheinberg War Cemetery. A 33-year-old married man from York, Sergeant Jackett had enlisted at the start of the war and was obviously a highly regarded air gunner. Due to the confusion and lack of information his wife, Ellen, received only news that he had been posted missing believed killed after failing to return from operations, along with a letter from his commanding officer. It was not until 4 May 1944 that his status was changed to presumed killed meaning that a death certificate could be issued and his personal items returned to his next of kin and it was not until close to the end of the war that his fate was confirmed. In the meantime, his wife was informed that her late husband had been awarded the DFM for the courage he had shown on operations, this award being gazetted on 28 July 1944 (his pilot was awarded the DFC).

At the age of 30, Flying Officer John Fort was older than most aircrew in Bomber Command but he had significant experience in the RAF. Although born in the Lancashire town of Colne he had moved to York with his parents before joining the RAF in 1929 as an apprentice at RAF Halton. After graduating as a fitter (he won first prize in his year) he had served on the ground and on the sea aboard HMS

Glorious. He had volunteered for aircrew duties in 1941 and trained as a bomb aimer. Once again, he had shown his abilities and was offered a commission. After OTU he was posted to No. 207 Squadron as part of the crew of Flight Lieutenant W. Elder. Unfortunately, his pilot was lost on a second-dickie trip at the end of February 1943 and, a month later, Fort and his crewmates were transferred to No. 97 Squadron where they linked up with Flight Lieutenant David Maltby DFC, an experienced pilot about to embark on his second operational tour. Maltby almost immediately volunteered to fly with a newly-formed squadron and took his new, and inexperienced, crew with him.

On the night of 16/17 May the majority of Bomber Command had been stood down due to the moon conditions, but one squadron was about to write its name in the history books for it was on this night that No. 617 Squadron undertook the dams raid. The news of the successful raid was greeted with joy in York and was almost the sole topic of conversation for a day or two. Few if any knew that a York airmen had played a key role in the attack on the Mohne Dam. Pilot Officer Fort was the bomb aimer in the aircraft of Flight Lieutenant David Maltby and was in the first wave of the attack. After the first four aircraft had attacked the Mohne without apparent success Maltby and his crew made their run. Fort, as bomb aimer, was a key member of the crew and he placed his bomb with great accuracy causing a large breach in the dam. The crew of J-Johnny were then told to return home and were the first to arrive back at base after successfully bombing. As a result, Pilot Officer Fort was awarded the DFC while a DSO and two DFMs were also awarded to other members of the crew.

The Allies had launched Operation Husky, the invasion of Sicily, on 9 July 1943. The fighting for the island had been ferocious but by 11 August the Germans had ordered the evacuation of their forces to the Italian mainland. The Allies had captured numerous airfields which were key to the support of the ground troops but these came under heavy aerial attack from the Luftwaffe. Defending the airfields were anti-aircraft units of the RAF Regiment. Amongst them was No. 2925

Squadron, which had been formed in May 1943 as a Light Anti-Aircraft unit (LAA), which had landed on the first day of the invasion and served at several captured airfields. By 11 August the squadron was defending the airfield near the newly captured town of Catania. The airfield came under repeated attack but the squadron helped to repel the Luftwaffe, though not without suffering casualties itself. Amongst them was a York Leading Aircraftman, Sidney Coe. The 20-year-old was the son of Dorothy Lonsborough and the foster son of Charles Lonsborough.[33]

As the attention of many in York focused on Bomber Command's campaign against Germany other York airmen were losing their lives in the struggle against Japan. The aircrew of No. 217 Squadron were taking part in anti-shipping strikes from airfields in Ceylon. These operations were mounted both in daylight and at night, could be very hazardous, and required a high degree of training. By August 1943 the squadron was equipped with both the Bristol Beaufort and the Beaufighter. On the night of 26 August the experienced crew of Flying Officer C. Watson were briefed to take part in a night torpedo practice attack on HMS *Scout*. The exercise was designed to give experience to a newly arrived pilot, Flying Officer R. Lund, and involved one Beaufort dropping flares while another launched its attack. One of the wireless operator/air gunners in the crew of Flying Officer Watson was York born Sergeant Frank Plows (23). The crew took off from RAF Vavuniya at 8:15pm and were over HMS *Scout* approximately three-quarters of an hour later. Aboard the ship observing were both flight commanders from No. 217 Squadron. They later reported how the Beaufort descended to approximately 1,500 feet before climbing sharply and then diving straight into the sea. Despite an immediate search which continued throughout the following day no bodies or wreckage was located.[34] Tragically, the accident claimed the lives of two York airmen as the 21-year-old Flying Officer Lund was also a native of the city.

One of the bright spots which had uplifted the morale of York was the news of the successful dams raid in May 1943. Since then

No. 617 Squadron had been relatively inactive although training had continued apace. On 14/15 September the squadron attempted to make an audacious low-level attack on the Dortmund-Ems Canal using the new 12,000lb bombs. The weather over the target was found to be poor and the squadron was recalled. The heavily loaded Lancasters turned around at low level before making their way home. The aircraft of dams raid veteran Flight Lieutenant D.J.H. Maltby DSO DFC, however, was seen to crash into the sea, killing all on board. His bomb-aimer, as ever, was Pilot Officer John Fort DFC.[35] The Lancashire airman's parents received the news of the loss of their son at their home in York.

For the people of York it had become commonplace to see reports of the death of local airmen in the newspapers or to hear from neighbours, family or friends that an acquaintance or loved one had been posted missing or had been killed. Despite this, the level of support for the operations of the RAF remained high and the nightly raids on Germany found widespread favour amongst the vast majority. On 5/6 September 1943 some 605 aircraft raided Mannheim and Ludwigshafen. The raid was a great success but at the cost of thirty-four aircraft which failed to return. At RAF Breighton the men and women of No. 78 Squadron suffered a heavy blow as four of their Halifaxes failed to return to base. Amongst them was Halifax II (JB872, EY-Q) which had taken off under the command of Pilot Officer F.C. Ebeling, RAAF. While the Halifax was on its bomb run at 19,000 feet it was attacked and damaged by a night fighter. The pilot decided to jettison some of his bombs short of the aiming point but to continue on to the target with the remainder. Damaged aircraft were always vulnerable and as the Halifax tried to return home both of its port engines failed and this caused the pilot to lose control as the bomber spun to the ground, killing all but one of the eight crew. The mid-upper gunner in the crew was Sergeant Walter Roy Huntley, a 22-year-old who left behind his young wife, Janet, in York.[36]

By this stage of the war the people of York were reading about ever-larger numbers of RAF bombers being sent to hit German towns and cities and the support for the efforts of the men in the bombers, many of whom spent some of their off-duty time in the city, was greatly appreciated, especially given the numbers of those losing their lives or being taken prisoner. The bomber airfields around York were home to the Halifax-equipped squadrons of No. 4 and No. 6 (RCAF) Group. By this stage the Halifax was suffering serious losses over the heavily defended German targets and many York families became accustomed to hearing that an airman friend or an entire crew that they had befriended had failed to return. As we have seen, large numbers of York men had been seduced by the perception of the glamour of serving in the RAF compared to the Army or Royal Navy and they paid a heavy price indeed.

On the night of 27/28 September a force of 678 bombers attacked Hanover but a faulty wind forecast resulted in much of the bombing falling in open countryside to the north of this important city. Even worse, some thirty-eight aircraft failed to return to their bases in England. At RAF Holme-on-Spalding Moor two aircraft from No. 76 Squadron failed to return. Halifax V (LK891, MP-X) had taken off at 7:09pm but nothing further was heard from the crew of Pilot Officer D.G. Griffiths and the Halifax and its crew disappeared without trace. The flight engineer in the crew was Sergeant Charles Raymond Walker, a 29-year-old York man.[37]

The activities of RAF Bomber Command, as we have seen, were greatly dependent upon the weather and the accurate forecasting of weather conditions for take-off, over Europe, over the target and back over England for when the bombers returned was of key importance. A number of methods were used including meteorological flights undertaken by a variety of units. Amongst them was No. 521 Squadron which operated a variety of aircraft types including the Gladiator biplane (for local reconnaissance), the Lockheed Hudson, and Handley-Page Hampdens which were no longer used by Bomber Command. On the night of 10 October 1943 Hampden TBI (L4202) was flying a reconnaissance over the North Sea (codenamed a RHOMBUS flight). The weather at RAF Docking was very poor and as the aircraft charged up the runway on its take-off it entered a dense fog bank and the pilot became disorientated. The Hampden swung off the runway and hit a gun post before bursting into flames. Amongst the crew who were killed was the navigator, Pilot Officer William Donald Cooper, aged 24, a married man from Heworth Green, York.[38]

For the York airmen who had flown early in the war there was little respite. After successfully completing a tour of duty they would be posted to various duties, usually as instructors, before being posted once more to an operational crew to undertake a further tour. Sergeant James Ferrie Craig had completed a tour as a wireless operator/air gunner with No. 58 Squadron in 1940-1941 and had been awarded a DFM on 17 January 1941. Sergeant Craig's pilot with No. 58 Squadron

Squadron Leader Clifford Wood. (Public Domain)

had been Clifford Wood (his pilot was mentioned in dispatches on the same day that Craig received his DFM) and August 1943 found him, as a flight sergeant, once more crewed up with the experienced and now promoted Squadron Leader Clifford S.F. Wood MiD, at No. 103 Squadron at RAF Elsham Wolds.

By 22 October the crew had flown fourteen operations together (a second tour for Flight Sergeant Craig and his pilot would have been twenty operations) and on the night of 22 October they were briefed, along with sixteen other crews from the squadron, for a raid on Kassel. The attack was undertaken by 569 aircraft and was a success. The accurate bombing resulted in a firestorm and a great deal of damage to this important target. The German night fighter tactics, however, were also successful and forty-three bombers failed to return to base. At No. 103 Squadron, three Lancasters were missing, amongst them was that of Squadron Leader Wood's crew. They had taken off shortly before 6 pm in Lancaster III (JB276, PM-F) but nothing more was heard from the crew. It was later established that the Lancaster had crashed at Wetschen at 9:30pm. Two of the crew (navigator and bomb-aimer) had managed to bale out to be taken prisoner but the other five, including Flight Sergeant Craig and Squadron Leader Wood were killed.[39]

With Germany's industry now increasingly desperate for raw materials the Royal Navy expended a great deal of effort in trying to stop blockade runners from reaching German ports. In October 1943 the British became aware of a blockade runner named *Munsterland* which was attempting to reach Germany with a cargo of latex and strategic metals. The Dido-Class cruiser HMS *Charybdis*, along with six destroyers, was assigned to search, locate and destroy *Munsterland*. On 22 October, however, a torpedo boat which was part of the blockade runner's escort hit HMS *Charybdis* with two torpedoes. The cruiser sank within half an hour with the loss of more than 400 of her crew; there were just 107 survivors. Amongst those whose bodies were never recovered was Electrical Mechanic 4th Class James Frederick Thompson, a 36-year-old married man from York.[40]

HMS Charybdis. (Public Domain)

While the main focus of the public with regard to the RAF was firmly based upon the actions of Fighter and Bomber Command, there was considerable aerial activity in the other theatres of war too. On 1 November 1943 the press reported that No. 27 Squadron, one of the RAF's Bristol Beaufighter squadrons in Burma, had achieved the feat of destroying or putting out of action 100 Japanese locomotives. The tally was reached after York airman Flight Sergeant Ronald D. Thorogood had taken off from Agartala on a daylight sweep beyond the Irrawaddy River. Flight Sergeant Thorogood described the attack, stating that he was flying at very low level along a single line track when he saw two engines pulling a mix of carriages and wagons. Thorogood immediately attacked with cannons and machine-guns, saw one engine blow up and believed that the other was also hit. On the same sortie Flight Sergeant Thorogood attacked a further four engines, seeing one of them belching smoke and flames as a result of his attack. The flight sergeant was the son of a York Police Constable. He had lived at Siward Street and had been educated at the Priory School and the School of Commerce before working as a clerk at the National Glass Works. He had volunteered for the RAF in 1940 and trained as a pilot in Canada before being posted to Egypt and then India.

The commanding officer of No. 27 Squadron was Wing Commander James Brindley Nicolson VC. Although born in London, Nicolson lived at Kirby Wharfe, close to York, and had been the only airman from Fighter Command to be awarded the VC during the Battle of Britain, while serving with No. 249 Squadron.[41] After recovering from the injuries he had sustained in 1940 he had been posted to India in 1942 and had taken command of No. 27 Squadron in August 1943. Wing Commander Nicolson had immediately proven himself in his new role and had been credited with having destroyed eleven locomotives in just one day.

By mid-December 1943 Bomber Command was engaged in the Battle of Berlin. Casualties mounted almost immediately as the

Wing Commander Nicolson VC, (centre) at hospital recuperating in 1940. (Public Domain)

German defences recovered from their blows earlier in the year and weather conditions worsened. These losses were exacerbated by the heavy defences around Berlin and the distance of the target from the RAF bases. On the night of 16/17 December a raid on the capital was made by 483 Lancaster bombers accompanied by ten Mosquitoes. Once again the German response was ferocious and well executed and, although the attack was reasonably accurate, some twenty-five Lancasters were lost along with another twenty-nine when upon return they found their bases covered with low cloud and fog. At RAF Ludford Magna two aircraft failed to return and another two crashed. Lancaster I (DV299, SR-K2) had taken off with Flight Sergeant P.E. Head at the controls but was lost without trace. The crew's flight engineer was Sergeant Wilfred Welby, a 21-year-old native of York. In his hometown his young wife, Patricia, and his parents, Wilfred and Florence, were notified that he had failed to return from operations but it was not until March 1945 that his status was changed to presumed killed.[42]

Mid-December 1943 also brought the news that a York airman, Sergeant George Morris, had been awarded the British Empire Medal (BEM) for gallant and distinguished service over Burma. Sergeant Morris had been a bricklayer prior to his enlistment in the RAF.

With the RAF fighting in every theatre across the globe it was necessary to move large amounts of aircraft, men and matériel around the world. This was an arduous task and a large portion of the burden was borne by RAF Transport Command. The Ferry Units which moved aircraft and men about required skilled crews and a number of Ferry Training Units (FTU) were created. Amongst them was No. 311 FTU which had been formed in May 1943 and was based at RAF Moreton-in-Marsh, but which flew from a number of satellite fields. The unit was responsible for ferrying Wellington bombers out to the Middle East and this task required not only good piloting, but also accurate navigation and careful fuel conservancy. On 18 December 1943 a crew from No. 311 FTU were undertaking a cross-country navigation and fuel consumption test flight. At 2:08pm witnesses at RAF Atcham saw the Wellington III (BK132) come out of cloud in a vertical dive with the engines screaming and strips of fabric ripping from the wings. The bomber crashed with massive force on the perimeter track of the airfield, blowing a military policeman off his feet. All of the five-man crew were killed instantly. The rear gunner in the Wellington was Sergeant David Hartnoll Wright, another York airman, aged just 20 at the time of his death.[43]

A York seaman lost his life in an accident on 21 February 1944. Able Seaman Arthur Baden Fletcher (21) was serving aboard the destroyer HMS *Onslow*. At the time of his death the destroyer was being refitted on the River Tyne. Able Seaman Fletcher was the son of Albert and Jenny Fletcher, and was buried at Preston Cemetery, Tynemouth.

Although the news of the D-Day landings brought a sense of excitement to the people of York and a hope that this was yet another sign of the beginning of the end, the majority of the population were keenly aware that a long struggle lay ahead of the Allied forces. For others, the anxiety was more intense as they suspected that a loved one might have been directly involved in the great invasion, a period of anxious waiting began as they waited for news. For some the news was terrible.

Sergeant John Cappleman was a 26-year-old married man from York and had lived at Maple Grove in the city before his wartime service. By 1944 Cappleman was serving as a Sergeant in No. 48 (Royal Marine) Commando. His unit was the final commando unit formed during the war and was a part of 4th Special Service Brigade. During the D-Day landings the brigade was tasked with landing on Juno Beach and taking several villages before capturing and holding the radar station at Douvres. No. 48 Commando landed and captured the villages of Saint-Aubin-sur-Mer and, after heavy fighting, Langrune-sur-Mer. The unit suffered heavy losses during this assault and afterwards dug in awaiting the arrival of reinforcements and heavy equipment. At some point during the fighting on this day Sergeant Cappleman was killed. His wife, Dorothy Vera Cappleman, and his parents, Barker and Beatrice-Ann Cappleman, received the news in York and his loss was published in a list of casualties in the local press towards the end of the month.[44]

The 1st Royal Norfolk Regiment was tasked with landing on Sword Beach before pushing on to take the strategically vital city of Caen. In the event the operation proved to be unsuccessful and the Norfolks and their supporting units were pinned down while still some miles short of their objective. The Norfolks suffered heavy casualties during the day as they attempted to advance against a ferocious defence from well dug-in and determined German units. Amongst those killed during the abortive attempt to take Caen was 19-year-old Private James Hudson. His mother, Ada Gertrude Hudson, was from York and she was clearly bereft at the loss of her son. After he was buried at , she had the following inscription placed upon his headstone: 'FORGOTTEN BY SOME IN THIS WORLD YOU MAY BE NEVER, MY DARLING, FORGOTTEN BY ME. MOTHER'.

One of the crucial factors in the invasion plan was the accurate direction of artillery, naval gunfire and aerial bombardment used to support the invasion forces. In order to do this, specialised soldiers from a variety of units were brought into the invasion alongside the early paratrooper and glider landings. Many of these men were drawn from a variety of units of the Royal Artillery. The paratroopers were particularly vulnerable to counter-attack from heavy enemy units and required the support of these forward observers. Amongst them was Captain Richard Stanley Bellerby of the Royal Artillery. Captain Bellerby, a native of York, was attached to 3 Parachute Brigade on D-Day and was amongst a group of Forward Observation Officers (FOO). As part of No. 125 FOO Party, Captain Bellerby and four other ranks boarded Airspeed Horsa glider (no. 125) at Tarrant Rushton in the early hours of D-Day. At 1:45am the glider took off, towed by a Halifax V of 298 Squadron, carrying the five men of 125 FOO along with the two sergeant pilots of the glider, a jeep and trailer and a motorcycle. The target for 125 FOO was to land at Drop Zone/Landing Zone N near to Ranville at 3:20am as part of the third wave of airborne troops in Operation Tonga. As the glider approached the French coast, however, it was hit by anti-aircraft fire and forced to crash-land in the sea. All on board were killed.[45] Captain Bellerby was the eldest son of Councillor G.S Bellerby and following his education at Malvern and Repton he had worked as a chartered accountant and had been a founder member of the Yorkshire branch of the Old Reptonians' Association. Captain Bellerby was initially reported missing and it was not until the end of October 1944 that his family were notified that he was believed to have lost his life on 6 June.

Another crucial part of the landings was the armoured units of the Royal Armoured Corps. Those landing with the first wave of troops were to provide crucial support at a time when the Allies had otherwise only light infantry on the beaches. The Nottinghamshire Yeomanry (Sherwood Rangers) were equipped with both swimming 'DD' Sherman tanks and non-swimming Shermans which were carried by landing craft. The tank crews paid a heavy price in fulfilling their

An Airspeed Horsa glider under tow. (Public Domain)

duties as they were targeted by enemy anti-tank guns. Amongst those to lose their lives was Trooper William John Hewlett of 'B' Troop (31) who left a widow, Edith, in York.[46]

At 4:30am on 6 June the men of 2nd Battalion East Yorkshire Regiment were packed aboard the MV *Empire Battleaxe* and HMS *Glenearn*. The men clambered down the sides of the ships into their landing craft and at 6am set off towards their landing zone on Queen Red Beach, a sector of Sword Beach. Landing under heavy artillery, mortar and machine-gun fire, the men of the East Yorks pushed on to attack a number of enemy strongpoints which housed artillery pieces. By 6pm the East Yorks and their supporting units had successfully taken strongpoints Cod and Sole in addition to the heavily defended Daimler Battery. After this the East Yorks pushed on to the village of St Aubin d'Arquenay where they were relieved by the King's Own Scottish Borderers. D-Day had cost the East Yorks five officers and sixty other ranks killed along with a further four officers and 137 other ranks wounded.

They were again in action the following day and throughout the Normandy campaign. The confused nature of the fighting meant that the dates of death of some of the East Yorks were not accurately established and the parents of 19-year-old Private Desmond Byers received news that their son had lost his life on either 6 or 7 June. Clearly proud of their son's sacrifice they had the following placed upon his headstone in Hermanville War Cemetery: 'HE SLEEPS WITH ENGLAND'S HEROES IN THE WATCHFUL CARE OF GOD.'

To support the invasion a number of specialised RAF squadrons were utilised. Amongst them was No. 69 Squadron which had been formed as a reconnaissance squadron in Malta in 1941 and was brought back to Britain especially for Operation Overlord. The squadron re-equipped with the obsolescent but adaptable Vickers Wellington bomber and was given a variety of night reconnaissance tasks, alongside dropping flares to support operations on the night of D-Day and to locate German troop movements at night. On the night of 6 June Wellington XIII (JA 619) was in difficulty and was struggling back to its base, the aircraft had suffered an engine failure and a decision was made by the crew to divert and to land at RAF Wratting Common (which was home to 1661 Heavy Conversion Unit). As they approached, the runway controller used his Aldis lamp to try to deny the crew permission to land but this was ignored, and the Wellington made a wheels-up belly landing. As the aircraft skidded along, it crashed into Stirling (BF 470) of 1651 HCU and the two aircraft burst into flames with two of the Wellington crew being killed. Amongst the crew of the No. 69 Squadron Wellington to lose their lives was Flight Sergeant Cyril John Gubbins, a 28-year-old York man. The airman had married Renee Jane Gubbins in 1940 and the couple had a young daughter, named after her mother.[47]

The men of the Home Guard had given very worthwhile service in York from their initial formation as the LDV in 1940 and for one NCO this service was recognised nationally in the King's birthday honours list of June 1944. Battery Quartermaster Sergeant (QMS) Frederick Barber received the British Empire Medal (BEM) as a reward for his services.

With the Home Guard being stood down there was great interest in the stand-down parade which took place in December 1944. The parade consisted of men and equipment from the 11th, 12th, 13th and 14th West Riding Battalions, No. 108 Yorkshire Home Guard Anti-Aircraft Battery, and the bands of the 14th West Riding and West Yorkshire Regiment. In total, more than 2,000 officers and men took part. Commanding Officer, Lieutenant General Sir Edwin L. Morris, and more than forty other ranking officers inspected the men after they were drawn up in the Museum Gardens. Morris read out the King's order of the day before giving his own farewell speech in which he spoke of his pleasure in being able to say farewell to the men who had served Yorkshire and the north of England so well since the creation of the force in 1940. The parade through the city culminated with the salute being taken at Clifford's Tower with General Morris being joined by the Lord Mayor (Councillor H.C. de Burgh), City Sheriff (Councillor J.H.

Kaye), Air Vice - Marshal C.R. Carr (of No. 4 Group, RAF Bomber Command), Sir Francis Terry and a number of civil defence leaders.

The fighting to liberate Belgium, France and Holland was fierce and many York soldiers found themselves in the forefront of it as the Allied armies attempted to push the Germans out of the occupied countries and advance into Germany. By January 1945 the Allies were in a position to begin preparing the way for the invasion of Germany. These preparations included the hugely dangerous task of seeking to clear a path through the extensive minefields which had been laid on the frontier as part of the German defences. The Dutch border town of Brunssum was headquarters to the 52nd (Lowland) Division and in the first week of January a large number of men from the Royal Engineers were engaged in mine clearance near to the town. The operation to clear the mines during this week claimed the lives of fifty soldiers and their bodies were brought back to the small military cemetery which had been created in the town in 1944. Amongst them were at least two York soldiers who lost their lives on the same day. Sapper Leonard Raymond Allison was just 21 when he died serving with No. 241 Field Company, Royal Engineers. Private Alan Feasby (18) serving with the 4th Battalion King's Own Scottish Borderers was killed in action on the same day as Sapper Allison.

While many York men found themselves on the front lines, others were still at home in Britain training before they were sent abroad. The Army had continued to expand and the training demands sometimes resulted in tragedy. A large number of young men who joined up lost their lives in accidents, whether in training or merely as a result of misadventure. On 17 January 1945 18-year-old Private Ronald Herbert Winteringham, known as 'Bud', was killed in an accident while serving with the Durham Light Infantry but on attached duty with the 10th Duke of Wellington's (West Riding Regiment). Ronald and nine other soldiers were swept to their deaths in the River Coquet at Guyzance, Northumberland, while attempting to practise river crossing despite warnings from locals that the river, which was in winter flood, was too high to make the attempt.[48]

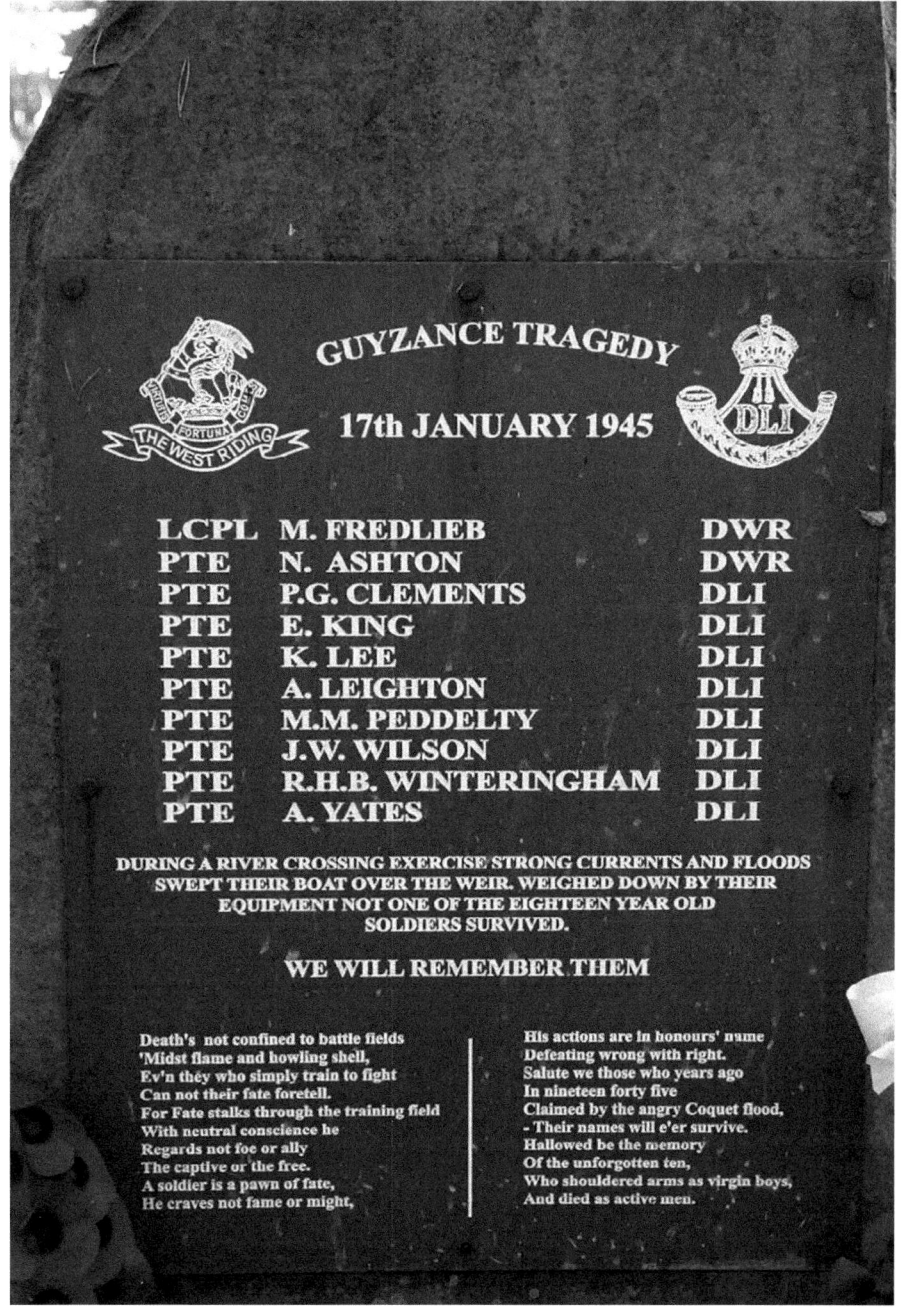

Memorial stone and plaque to the victims of the Guyzance tragedy. (Author's Collection)

On 8 February 1945 another married York soldier lost his life. Private Arthur Patrick Peart was aged 29 and serving in the Pioneer Corps when he died.[49] As the Allied armies began to penetrate the Dutch-German border in February and March 1945 the fighting grew even more fierce and casualties began to mount. As a result a number of families in York received the telegram that every family feared in wartime Britain. Lieutenant Fred Williams was a 28-year-old officer serving with the East Yorkshire Regiment attached to the 2nd Seaforth Highlanders when he was killed in action on 10 February in fighting around the area of the Dutch village of Mook. His wife, Marjorie Enid Williams, received the news at their York home.[50]

The Hallamshire Battalion of the York and Lancaster Regiment had been involved in the fighting in Holland throughout the entire campaign and by late February was manning positions close to the Dutch-German border. The Germans had flooded much of the area and on 20 February the battalion was ordered to send men to occupy a farm at De Hoeven. The farm was surrounded by water up to five foot in depth and, because of the nearby German positions, was only approachable by boat at night. One of the boats was hit by an explosion, most likely a mine, and eight men were killed and several wounded. Amongst those killed was Private George Alfred Yorke, a York native aged just 18. Private Edward McNichol (20) of York was wounded on the same night (most likely in the same incident). The young soldier died of his wounds two days later.[51]

The U-boat menace was also one which continued to claim the lives of York service personnel right up until the last days of the war. On the night of 24 February the Anti-Submarine Warfare (ASW) Trawler HMS *Ellesmere* was escorting a convoy of landing craft to Malta and was off Brest when she was hit by a torpedo. The resultant explosion completely destroyed the trawler and killed all of the thirty-three people on board. An escort which went to the site of the sinking found only splintered rafts and an upturned whaler. Amongst the dead was Stoker Joseph Edward Waiting (28), the son of Joseph and Ethel who lived in York.[52]

HMS Ellesmere. (Public Domain)

As we have seen, many of the families of York men who were lost in action faced an anxious wait for information as to their fate, but for a large number this confirmatory news never came and the families and friends faced the agonies of never truly knowing what had befallen the missing and the lack of a body or remains preyed upon the thoughts of many.

In March 1945 the Germans were attempting to evacuate their remaining forces from northern Italy in order to bolster the defences of Germany itself. The RAF made desperate attempts to halt the retreat by mounting bombing operations against enemy transport and the road, rail and harbour facilities which the Germans were using. At Rimini the Spitfire IXs of 111 Squadron had been converted to a fighter-bomber role and were amongst those taking part in the bombing operations. On the morning of 5 March Warrant Officer John Henry Coates should have been on leave but he had agreed to take on the duties of a comrade and fly a bombing operation with five other Spitfire pilots. The target of the operation was a number of barges moored on a canal close to the village of Cavarzere on the outskirts of Venice. The Spitfires of Treble

One found and bombed the target amidst heavy anti-aircraft fire, but one of them was hit and reported to have crashed and exploded on the ground. The pilot was Warrant Officer Coates, a native of York, born in 1921. His parents, John Eliza, lived at Eight Avenue in Tang Hall and his father worked as a confectionary maker at Rowntrees. Before joining the RAF Warrant Officer Coates, known to family and friends as Harry, had worked as a draughtsman for the LNER. This was a reserved occupation but Harry decided that he wished to do his bit and joined the RAF to train as a pilot. His family in York, consisting of his parents, three brothers and three sisters, received the news that Harry had been posted missing but nothing further was heard and the Coates family knew only that he had been reported shot down in northern Italy.

Bomber Command's war continued until the very end and a number of York airmen lost their lives in the final weeks of the war. On the night of 7/8 March the main raid was on Dessau but other large forces were sent to Hemmingstadt and Harburg. The Hemmingstadt force consisted of 281 bombers (mainly Halifaxes from No. 4 and 6 Groups). The target was an oil refinery and the raid cost the command five aircraft. Amongst the four Halifaxes that were lost were two from No. 578 Squadron. The flight engineer in Halifax III (NR150, LK-P) flown by Flight Lieutenant K. Shaw was Sergeant Kenneth Relton, a 19-year-old native of York. The Shaw crew were heard calling for help on wireless at 10:24 but the aircraft seemingly crashed into the sea shortly thereafter.[53]

At the end of March 1945 the Allies had successfully crossed the Rhine during Operation Plunder. The action had been very fierce with the Allies suffering almost 7,000 casualties during the crossing and subsequent fighting to establish and defend a beachhead. The 1st Battalion Cheshire Regiment had been at the forefront and continued to be engaged immediately afterwards. Due to the ferocity of the fighting it was taking some time to notify relatives and it was May 1945 before Mabel Cawley received a telegram which notified her that her husband, Private Sidney Joseph Cawley (32), had been killed in action on 14 April while serving with the Cheshire Regiment.[54] The personal inscription on the York-born soldier's grave read:

AT THE GOING DOWN OF THE SUN AND IN THE MORNING WE WILL REMEMBER THEM R.I.P.

The 1st battalion of the Rifle Brigade had been involved in the fighting in Europe since D-Day and suffered heavy casualties as a result. At Dringhouses in York, Major Francis A. Robinson and his wife, Ethel Mary Robinson, received a telegram informing them that their 21-year-old son Lieutenant Michael Henry Aidan Robinson had been killed in action on 1 April.[55]

The end of March 1945 also saw the Allies launch their final offensive in Italy. The wet winter weather had meant that little or no concerted action had been possible on the plains through the winter but March saw the preparatory engagements before Operation Grapeshot was launched. Captain Kenneth Austin Griffith, aged 24, was with the Royal Armoured Corps serving on attachment to the headquarters of the Sixth Armoured Division at the time. Griffith was a Liverpudlian who lived in Blackpool but he had married a York woman, Moira Mary Griffith. He had been commissioned as a lieutenant in 1942 but had obviously proven his worth. The events surrounding his death are somewhat unclear and it appears that he may have died in an accident with his date of death being given as either 24 or 25 March.[56]

As Bomber Command's long and arduous war neared its end casualties had declined from the slaughter which had been suffered from 1942 to early 1944, but they were still severe enough to make headlines and for those York families with loved ones flying on the front lines the worry was every bit as intense as earlier in the war. The command was now capable of sending forces to raid several targets in a night and on the night of 4/5 April targets included Leuna, Harburg and Lutzkendorf. Substantial 'mining' operations were also undertaken with thirty Lancasters from No. 1 Group laying mines in the waters in the Oslo Fjord and the Kattegat. Tragically, three of the Lancasters failed to return from this operation. Two of these were from No. 153 Squadron. One was flown by the squadron's commanding officer, while the other was flown by Flight Lieutenant A.J. Winder. This Lancaster I (NX563, P4-R) had taken off from RAF Scampton and vanished without trace. The mid-upper gunner in the crew was Flying Officer Arthur Samuel Blake, a married man from Heworth, York.[57]

January through to March saw the Allied forces in Burma on the offensive as the Fourteenth Army attempted to capture first

A Sherman tank (of the 63rd Motorised Bgd) advances towards Meiktila. (Public Domain)

Meiktila and then Mandalay. The Battle of Meiktila was very hard fought as the Allied forces first took the town and then had to stand against determined Japanese efforts to recapture it. The Fourteenth Army was a multinational force with large contingents of soldiers from Britain, India and Africa. Amongst the armoured units which were part of the force fighting at Meiktila was Probyn's Horse (The 5th King Edward's Own Lancers), Indian Armoured Corps, which was part of the 255th Indian Tank Brigade equipped with American Sherman tanks. Keith Swindells was a 20-year-old native of York who had been given an emergency commission as a second lieutenant in April 1944, but by the time of the Battle of Meiktila had been promoted to lieutenant; he was killed in action on 17 March 1945.[58]

The men of the 1st and 2nd battalions of the West Yorkshire Regiment spent the entire war in the Far East and both battalions served throughout the Burma Campaign. By the end of March 1945 the Fourteenth Army had captured both Meiktila and Mandalay and by the first week of April they were preparing the way for a two-pronged attack down the Irrawaddy and Sittang Rivers. This preparatory phase saw the death in action of another York soldier when Private Arthur March (33) was killed on 6 April while serving with the 1st Battalion West Yorks.[59]

Even as the war in Europe entered its final days the hostilities continued on land, in the air and at sea. On 29 April 1945 the Captain-class frigate HMS *Goodall* was escorting a convoy in the Barents Sea and was off the entry to the Kola Inlet when she came under attack from two U-boats. At 10pm a torpedo fired from *U-286* hit *Goodall* with devastating effect. The ammunition magazine exploded and blew the forward half of the ship clean off. The captain and many of the crew were killed while the sixty-one survivors abandoned ship and were picked up. Amongst those to lose their lives was a 20-year-old York-born seaman, telegraphist Raymond Mawson, whose parents, Herbert and Rachel, lived in York.[60]

Indian troops of the Punjab Rifles advance under cover of a Sherman tank during the Battle of Meiktila. (Public Domain)

Even after the end of the war in Europe there were still dangers and the arrival of a telegram for Mrs Kitty Shaw of Heworth, York, must have had a particularly tragic impact as it informed her that her husband, Bombardier George Albert Shaw (32), had died in the vicinity of Hamburg on 11 May.[61]

CHAPTER 4

Conclusion

We have already covered the story of how Warrant Officer Harry Coates had been shot down in his Spitfire over northern Italy in March 1945. His family had received no news other than that Harry had reportedly been shot down by anti-aircraft fire and had been posted missing believed killed. In 2017, however, a group called the Romagna Air Finders who specialised in locating and excavating crash sites from the Second World War were mounting a dig on a crash site close to Cavarzere when a local who had witnessed the Spitfire spiralling to the earth related the story to one of the archaeologists who mounted a second dig. This dig uncovered the wreckage of Spitfire IX PT410, buried 27 feet deep in clay which had preserved the remains to a very high degree. The wreckage included the engine, wings, cockpit, parts of the fuselage and an amount of ammunition. In the wreckage of the cockpit were the remains of the pilot. Checks showed that the remains were those of Warrant Officer John Henry 'Harry' Coates. The Romagna Air Finders began a wide-ranging appeal to try to find surviving relatives of the pilot and members of the Coates family saw the news coverage before getting in contact.

Sadly, Harry's last surviving siblings had died in the years before the discovery of his remains but members of the extended family of Warrant Officer Coates were invited to the funeral ceremony which took place in Cavarzere. There, the family were shocked and gratified by the outpouring of gratitude and respect accorded to Harry Coates. Fully 500 locals turned out for the ceremony, in which Warrant Officer Coates was buried with full military honours, at the church in Cavarzere with the Mayor of Cavarzere thanking him for his sacrifice in helping to liberate Italy. A moving burial ceremony then took place at Padua War Cemetery with a great-great niece and great-great nephew laying white roses on

Warrant Officer John Henry 'Harry' Coates, RAF. (Daily Mail)

his coffin. Talking to the press after the funeral two of Warrant Officer Coates' family told how the loss of Harry had affected the family.

Niece, Mrs Shelagh Coates, said 'The sadness I feel is for his six siblings, including my father Frank who died in 2015. They all survived the war and always longed for him to be found, but they all died before it happened.'[1] Another niece, Mrs Christine Stanton, said that her mother, Harry's sister, 'never came to terms with Harry's death. She died in 2008. But today was the most beautiful service, conducted with great dignity, and it brought a lot of closure. I felt very proud of him.'[2] Mrs Coates, talking about the ceremony, added that 'It was overwhelming to see so many here for a man they never knew. One lady said she came for what he did – fighting for their freedom.'[3]

After the burial a Commonwealth War Grave Commission headstone was erected for Warrant Officer Coates and his family had the following inscription placed upon it:

'BLUE SKIES FOREVER REST IN PEACE HARRY, NEVER FORGOTTEN BY FAMILY'.

The deaths of three members of the Moll family at their farm at Dunnington Lodge in the early hours of 4 March 1944 when a German night fighter crashed into their home was also remembered and on 19 June 1993 a cross was erected and dedicated at the site. The cross was dedicated to all of those who died (including the four Luftwaffe airmen) and wreaths were laid by a representative of the Luftwaffe

Warrant Officer Coates standing on the wing of a Spitfire. (Daily Mail)

Night Fighter Association and by Mr Arthur Tait, a Halifax rear gunner who had been wounded on the night in question.

York may not have experienced the extended bombing that other communities went through during the war and some may have believed the city to have been somewhat isolated from the war, but the heavy attack on the city in April 1942, other minor attacks, the contribution of York industries to the war effort and the sacrifices made by men and women from York who served in the forces meant that the people of York experienced the war in every way. The recovery and burial of the remains of Harry Coates and the commemoration of the Moll family demonstrate that the people of York will not forget the sacrifices made by their fellow residents during the Second World War. It is fitting that such men and women are remembered.

Endnotes

Chapter 1: Civilians at War

1. *Leeds Mercury*, 23 October 1939, p.3.
2. A heavier attack was made on the same night on Tyneside and Northumberland but, again, little damage was done.
3. *Yorkshire Post & Leeds Intelligencer*, 16 August 1940, p. 6.
4. *Yorkshire Post*, 12 August 1941, p. 6.
5. *Yorkshire Post*, 22 August 1941, p. 6.
6. *Yorkshire Post*, 26 August 1941, p. 5.
7. *Yorkshire Post*, 1 May 1942, p. 6.
8. *Bradford Observer*, 25 September 1942, p. 3.
9. *Yorkshire Post and Leeds Intelligencer*, 18 December 1942, p. 1.
10. Two of the raiders were later confirmed as having crashed. Dornier Do217E (4342) crashed into a hillside near Hemsley killing all four crew while Dornier Do217E (4348) crashed into a hillside near Pickering, again killing all four crew.
11. There are approximately 600 names on the mirror, many those of men who failed to return from operations.
12. P/O Low spent many months in hospital but met his future wife in one of the nurses who nursed him back to help. Mr Hardcastle's leg injury was so severe that the leg had to be amputated.

Chapter 2: Blitz – The Air Raid of 28/29 April 1942

1. *Fife Free Press & Kirkcaldy Guardian*, 18 July 1942, p. 4.
2. Mahe and his brother had escaped France to carry on the fight and the courageous W/O Mahe later received a civic welcome at the Mansion House in honour of his actions over York that night.

Chapter 3: Military Service

1. F.Lt Dodds, MiD, is commemorated on the Runnymede Memorial.
2. Fusilier Eckersley is buried at Merville Communal Cemetery Extension.
3. *Yorkshire Post & Leeds Intelligencer*, 9 August 1940, p. 6.
4. Sgt Crane is commemorated on the Runnymede Memorial.
5. Sgt Gray is buried at Fulford Cemetery.
6. Lieutenant Kirkup is commemorated on the Plymouth Naval Memorial. HMS *Warwick Deeping* was also sunk in the action.
7. Stoker 1st Class Sproat is commemorated on the Chatham Naval Memorial.
8. A/S Day is commemorated in the Chatham Naval Memorial.
9. Mess Room Boy Brown is commemorated on the Tower Hill Memorial.
10. P/O Dales is buried at Fulford Cemetery.
11. Steward Hartley is commemorated on the Plymouth Naval Memorial. The survivor from HMS *Perseus* was one of two passengers who were hitching a ride to Alexandria. Leading Stoker John Capes was one of four men who escaped the submarine using Davis Submerged Escape Apparatus but only he survived the ascent and five mile swim to the island of Cephalonia. He was hidden here by islanders for eighteen months before he was smuggled to Turkey. Capes was awarded the British Empire Medal for his exploits. When the wreck was surveyed in 1997 it was confirmed that the probable cause of loss was a mine.
12. The battle ended the Allied naval efforts in SE Asia for 1942 as the vast majority of available forces had been sunk or damaged and forced to flee.
13. Amongst these losses was HMS *Exeter*, badly damaged during the Battle of the Java Sea she was sunk the next day as she attempted to flee to Australia.
14. A/S Smith is commemorated on the Portsmouth Naval Memorial.
15. CPO Preston is commemorated on the Plymouth Naval Memorial.
16. Motor Mechanic Snowball is commemorated on the Chatham Naval Memorial.

17. *The Press*, 20 April 2007.

18. A/S Shaw is commemorated on the Portsmouth Naval Memorial.

19. A/S Taylor is commemorated on the Chatham Naval Memorial.

20. AC2 Ward is buried in his hometown at York Cemetery.

21. The dead were: Cpl Herbert Hanson (33), of 11 Nursery Street, Birkby, Huddersfield; AC1 Dennis Smollan (22), of Jesmond, Newcastle; AC1 Albert J James (21), of 64 Ashvale Place, Aberdeen; Sgt (Air Gunner) George Bernard Noble(24) of Foulsyke Farm, Fylingdale, Robin Hood's Bay; Sgt James T .Tremain (22), of 71 Warwick Road, Batley; Sgt Leonard G Moseley (23), of Weston Road, Mickleover, Derby; AC2 Norman Ward (21), of 251 Tang Hall Lane, York; and AC2 Herbert Larman (19) of 263 Levy Street, Radcliffe, Lancs. AC1 Smollan was a Jew whose parents lived at Montreal in Canada. He is buried at Hazlerigg Jewish Cemetery. His older brother, Joshua (29), was killed when his Hudson was lost on 30 January 1944 over Italy and his younger brother, Harold (19) was killed in Germany on 7 April 1945 while serving with 7 Btn, Parachute Regiment.

22. Sgt Couldwell and his crew are commemorated on the Runnymede Memorial.

23. Sgt Gruntman and his crew are commemorated on the Runnymede Memorial. For the Black family the loss was particularly tragic as F/O Black's older brother, Sq/Ldr J.W. Black, RNZAF, had been lost on a previous Berlin operation on 7 November 1941. A third Black brother was serving in the UK but he was returned to New Zealand after this tragedy.

24. F/O Huggard and five of his crew are commemorated on the Runnymede Memorial while the body of his mid-upper gunner, Sgt J.H. Hughes, was washed up and is buried at Durnbach War Cemetery.

25. The crew of Sq/Ldr Hayward possessed between them two DFCs and three DFMs. They were: Sq/Ldr E.L. Hayward, DFC (pilot); Sgt G.W.F. Baker (flight engineer); F/Lt J.O. Young, DFC

(navigator); P/O A. Urquhart (bomb-aimer); P/O E.H. Mantle, DFM & Bar (wireless operator); F/Sgt G.V. Pryor, DFM (mid-upper air gunner); and Sgt D. Brown (rear air gunner). All are buried at Lichtenvoorde General Cemetery. This was the first Lancaster III from 106 Squadron to be lost on operations.

26. P/O Richmond and his crewmates lie in Abbeville Communal Cemetery Extension.

27. Sgt Abbot and his crew are all buried in Svino Churchyard. Bomber Command was a multi-national force but, unusually, this crew consisted of airmen from the RAF, RAAF, RCAF and the RNZAF.

28. F/Sgt Pugh's Lancaster had been shot down by a night fighter killing all seven of the crew. The bodies of at least three of the crew (the navigator and the two air gunners) were recovered and buried in a temporary cemetery but after the war were moved to Jonkerbos War Cemetery while F/Sgt Pugh and the remaining three crew are commemorated on the Runnymede Memorial.

29. Sgt Thompson is commemorated on the Runnymede Memorial.

30. Sgt Eaglen is buried at Eglantine All Saints Churchyard, County Down.

31. Sgt Gomersall and those of his crew who were killed lie in Hamburg Cemetery.

32. F/O Abbey is buried at Fulford Cemetery.

33. LAC Coe is buried at Catania War Cemetery. Interestingly, official documents describe LAC Coe as being a Navigator Observer.

34. Sgt Plows and his four comrades are commemorated on the Singapore Memorial. The cause of the crash was never established. Some reports erroneously claim structural failure but the official reports make no mention of this and the witnesses, including both flight commanders, describe that the engines sounded as though they were functioning normally. It is likely that the pilot became disorientated in the dark and the aircraft stalled as it began to climb.

35. The only body to be recovered was that of S/Ldr Maltby (who is buried at Wickhambreaux in Norfolk) while P/O Fort, DFC, and his

comrades are commemorated on the Runnymede Memorial. The crew were: S/Ldr D.J.H. Maltby, DSO, DFC (pilot); Sgt W. Hatton (flight engineer); F/Sgt V. Nicholson, DFC (navigator); F/O John Fort, DFC (bomb aimer); F/Sgt A.J. Stone (wireless operator); F/Sgt V.Hil (front gunner)l; W/O J.L. Welch, DFM (mid-upper gunner); and Sgt H.T. Simmonds (rear gunner). All but W/O Welch, who had been seconded from 218 Squadron, had flown with Maltby on the dams raid. The cause of the crash has never been resolved. Early claims focussed on the possibility that the Lancaster had been caught in the slipstream of another bomber but it is now believed that it may have been involved in a mid-air collision with a 139 Squadron Mosquito. 617 Squadron tried again the next night but the result was disastrous and five out of eight aircraft were lost, including that of the new commanding officer, S/Ldr G. Holden, DSO, DFC & bar, MiD (along with most of Gibson's dams raid crew), and dams raid veteran F/Lt L.G. Knight, DSO, MiD, RAAF, and crew.

36. Sgt Huntley is buried at Choloy War Cemetery, France.

37. Sgt Walker and his seven comrades are commemorated on the Runnymede Memorial.

38. P/O Cooper is buried at Berkswell Churchyard, Warwickshire.

39. The crew were: Sq/Ldr C.S.F. Wood, MiD (pilot); Sgt C. Kershaw (flight engineer); F/Lt W.H. Hopkns (navigator); F/Lt C.L. Grisdale (bomb-aimer); F/Sgt J.F. Craig, DFM (wireless operator); Sgt H.R. Wilson (mid-upper gunner); and Sgt W.R. Brown (rear gunner). F/Sgt Craig was posthumously promoted to Warrant Officer. All of the dead lie in Hanover War Cemetery.

40. Electrical Mechanic 4th Class Thompson is commemorated on the Plymouth Naval Memorial.

41. Wing Commander Nicolson was the only Battle of Britain pilot to be awarded the VC and was the only member of Fighter Command to receive the award during the Second world War. He was later awarded the DFC for his work with 27 Squadron but was killed

on 2 May 1945 when the B24 Liberator from 355 in which he was flying as an observer caught fire and crashed into the Bay of Bengal. Wing Commander Nicolson's body was not recovered and he is commemorated on the Singapore Memorial, he was 28. To commemorate the 75th anniversary of the Battle of Britain in 2015 the RAF painted a Typhoon jet in Second World War colours and applied Nicolson's squadron letters, GN-A, upon it.

42. Sgt Welby and his crew are commemorated on the Runnymede Memorial.

43. Sgt Wright is buried at Stockton-on-the-Forest (Holy Trinity) Churchyard.

44. Sgt Cappleman is buried at Bayeux War Cemetery.

45. Captain Bellerby's body was never recovered and he and four of his comrades are commemorated on the Bayeux Memorial. The bodies of Gunner R.T. Dennison (53 (The Worcestershire Yeomanry) Light Airlanding Light Regiment) and Gunner D. Simmons (2 Airlanding Light Anti-Aircraft Battery (attd. 53 Airlanding Light Regiment)) were washed up on the Normandy shore with the first mentioned being buried at Bayeux War Cemetery and the latter lying at Tilly-sur-Suelles War Cemetery.

46. Trooper Hewlett is buried ay Bayeux War Cemetery.

47. F/Sgt Gubbins is buried at Fulford Cemetery.

48. Pvt Winteringham is buried at York Cemetery.

49. Pvt Peart is buried at Leopoldsburg War Cemetery.

50. Lieutenant Williams lies in Mook War Cemetery.

51. Pvt Yorke is buried at Arnhem Oosterbeek War Cemetery while Pvt McNichol lies in Uden War Cemetery.

52. Stoker Waiting is commemorated on the Lowestoft Naval Memorial.

53. The body of the pilot was later washed up and he now lies in Kiel War Cemetery but Sgt Relton and the remainder of the crew are commemorated on the Runnymede Memorial.

54. Pvt Cawley is buried at Becklingen War Cemetery.

55. Lieutenant Robinson is buried at Reichswald War Cemetery.

56. Captain Griffith is buried at Coriano Ridge War Cemetery.
57. F/O Blake and his crew are commemorated on the Runnymede Memorial. According to W.R. Chorley both 153 Squadron Lancasters were shot down into the Kattegat by the night fighter of Major Werner Husemann. The commanding officer of 153 Squadron, W/Cdr F.S. Powley, DFC, AFC, had joined the RAF in 1936 and was a contemporary of W/Cdr G.P. Gibson.
58. Lieutenant Swindells is buried at Taukkyan War Cemetery.
59. Pvt March is buried at Taukkyan War Cemeetery.
60. Telegraphist Mawson's body was not recovered and he is commemorated on the Chatham Naval Memorial.
61. Bombardier Shaw is buried in Hamburg Cemetery.

Chapter 4: Conclusion

1. *Mail Online* [https://www.dailymail.co.uk/news/article-6855615/Spitfire-pilot-shot-killed-near-Venice-WWII-finally-laid-rest-74-years-later.html].
2. *Ibid*.
3. *Ibid*.

Index